Emotion-Focused
Cognitive Therapy

Emotion-Focused Cognitive Therapy

Mick Power

With assistance from
Pierre Philippot and Ursula Hess

A John Wiley & Sons, Ltd., Publication

Registered Office
John Wiley & Sons Ltd, The Atrium, Southern Gate, Chichester, West Sussex, PO19 8SQ, UK

Editorial Offices
The Atrium, Southern Gate, Chichester, West Sussex, PO19 8SQ, UK
9600 Garsington Road, Oxford, OX4 2DQ, UK
350 Main Street, Malden, MA 02148-5020, USA

For details of our global editorial offices, for customer services, and for information about how to apply for permission to reuse the copyright material in this book please see our website at www.wiley.com/wiley-blackwell.

Library of Congress Cataloging-in-Publication Data

Power, Michael J.
  Emotion focused cognitive therapy / Mick Power ; with assistance from Pierre Philippot and Ursula Hess.
    p. ; cm.
  Includes bibliographical references and indexes.
  Summary: "An academic text which clearly explains the theory of EFCT and its relationship with CBT. Provides a critique of CBT and other therapeutic approaches. Offers a summary of recent work on emotion, including an outline of the SPAARS approach. Written in an accessible manner, with trainee and practising therapists in mind. Presents the EFCT approach, with large numbers of clinical case examples summarised to reflect appropriate issues in working with emotions. Looks at the issues involved in working with problems related to the five basic emotions of fear, sadness, anger, disgust, and happiness"–Provided by publisher.
  ISBN 978-0-470-68323-1 (hardback) – ISBN 978-0-470-68322-4 (pbk.) 1. Emotion-focused therapy. 2. Cognitive therapy. I. Philippot, Pierre, 1960– II. Hess, Ursula, 1960– III. Title.
  [DNLM: 1. Cognitive Therapy–methods. 2. Emotions. 3. Mental Disorders–therapy. WM 425.5.C6 P887e 2010]
    RC489.F62P69 2010
    616.89′1425–dc22

                            2009043701

A catalogue record for this book is available from the British Library.

Typeset in 11.5/13.5pt Minion by Aptara Inc., New Delhi, India.
Printed in Singapore by Markono Print Media Pte Ltd.

1 2010

To Irina

Contents

List of Tables and Figures

Acknowledgements

A book about emotion and therapy should say something about the emotional life of its author as well as that of the many clients whose experiences it draws from. You will be relieved that this book is not an autobiography, though it does occasionally refer to my emotions in relation to some of my clients. However, an acknowledgements section in a book on emotion that did not acknowledge the author's emotions would seem incongruous and invite the same criticisms that our cultural bad-mouthing of emotion in favour of rationality receives throughout this book.

In fact, the past two or three years during which this book was written has been one of the most emotionally turbulent periods of my life, perhaps fittingly you might say. Personally, I have been through a separation and a divorce.

Lorna (my ex-wife) and Liam, Jack and Robyn (my children), I apologize for some of the painful emotions that I have put you through during this time. Sometimes it is necessary to experience pain in order to survive better in the long term, and I hope that we will manage this as well as we can. Thank you, Lorna Champion, Charlie Sharp, Tim Dalgleish, Andy MacLeod and Irina Astanina for your emotional and intellectual support during this time.

Perhaps it is unusual to mention in an acknowledgements section not only the people who helped with its production but also those who *hindered* its production. However, it is not just my personal life that has been in turmoil during the writing of this book but also my work life. I want to name those few people who have made both my work life and others' work lives so difficult over the past few years. Therefore, Karen MacKenzie, Jacqueline Wilson and Liz Bondi, I absolutely do not thank you for the difficulties you have caused during this time! There! It is interesting that simply having expressed these negative feelings leaves one feeling better! Of course, and this is one of the key messages of this book – express such negative feelings in a safe manner and preferably with people you feel close to and can trust! But express those feelings you must! So I thank you, kind reader, for allowing me this short outburst about my own life. Thank you too, Kath Melia, Ann Green, Dave Peck, Kathryn Quinn and Eleanor Sutton for your wonderful support during this time and for putting up with much longer outbursts from me. I hope I have managed to repay you all with some support because you have also had to survive the problems life has thrown at you.

Now back to the book! It might have been completed a year or two later, but it has benefitted from input from other colleagues and students. In particular, thank you, Ursula Hess, for your willingness to allow us to use your facial expression package for the training programme included with the book and Pierre Philippot for reading and commenting on the manuscript and your tireless work on the training package. Other colleagues who have made good contributions include Ken Laidlaw, Martin Eisemann and Somnath Chatterji. Thank you all, my students Katy Phillips, John Fox, Alexandra Dima, Amani Albrazi, Alexandra Skoropadskaya and Massimo Tarsia for many stimulating discussions on emotions and for your contributions to emotion research. And most of all, to you, Irina, to whom I dedicate this book.

1
Introduction

Psychology lost its soul at the beginning of the twentieth century with the joint onslaught of both American and Russian Behaviourism. As John Watson famously said, 'the soul is not the remit of science'. However, in the 1950s psychology at least regained its capacity to *think* – cognitive psychology was reputedly born at a symposium at the Massachusetts Institute of Technology on 11 September 1956 (see Bruner, 1983) and the subsequent development of cognitive science has swamped psychology and the many adjoining areas of linguistics, anthropology, philosophy and artificial intelligence. We should of course be grateful that we are no longer trapped in the one-dimensional world of behaviourism, in which we are no better than headless chickens (or pigeons, or rats) running around the farmyard, cage or Skinner Box. Cognitive science has at least given us more computational power – unfortunately, the behaviourist's computer would still have us using the abacus, or a mechanical equivalent.

And in the field of therapy, cognitive science has given us the many and varied cognitive and cognitive behavioural therapies. Yes, of course we should be grateful to be given back our *thinking* minds. At least the cognitive and cognitive behavioural therapies acknowledge that we have thoughts and beliefs and assumptions and schemas. It often makes sense to our clients that they may overvalue one thought at the expense of another, or they may have a mistaken belief about their own worthlessness as people, or they may believe that they are about to die of a heart attack when they are not. We know as clinicians that many of our clients can be helped by examining their cognitions and by examining the possibility that alternative cognitions would be more functional and would help them improve their well-being and general life satisfaction.

Cognitive science and cognitive behavioural therapies can absolutely be congratulated for the benefits they have brought to academics, to clinicians and to clients. But unfortunately something has been left out in these great strides forward – and that is *emotion*. There has been growing recognition in the past 20 years or so that cognition is not enough. We may now be able to produce computers that can play a good game of chess, but we are yet to see a computer commit suicide because it was rejected in love, or take out a gun and shoot someone because of an insult to its mother (or perhaps its *motherboard*?). Much of what we do as humans is motivated by emotion. We build a monument to the person we have loved and lost because we are overwhelmed with grief and want to find a way to express those emotions. We strive for wealth, fame and success because we believe those things will make us happy – whether or not they will – if or when we ever achieve them. We move to another country and learn to speak Russian because we fall in love. We avoid leaving the house at a certain time because we hate our neighbours, who leave rubbish in our drive-way because they hate us! We teach our children to look right and left as they cross the road because we are terrified of what might happen to them if they carelessly forget. The list of emotion-motivated things we do is endless. Emotion is constantly with us and guiding us, for that is its purpose. When emotions function well and properly, they help us to prioritize, to work when we would rather play, to choose between otherwise impossible choices, and to avoid situations and objects that might be dangerous or unhealthy or disease ridden. The well-functioning emotion system is there to guide and protect – emotions are the 10 commandments of the psychological world. But as any powerful system, the emotion system can run out of control. Danger can be signalled when there is no objective danger – the harmless spider in the bath really does not warrant that level of panic and disgust. Or, the person can be so overwhelmed by feelings of despair and self-disgust that he or she would rather be dead. Or, the driver cutting in front of us can instantly fill us with an inexplicable feeling of road rage that causes us to put lives in danger.

The purpose of this book, therefore, is to continue driving the tide of work that is beginning to appear on the importance of emotion. Our own view is that emotion and cognition (i.e. thinking and feeling) are intimately and inextricably tied together (Power & Dalgleish, 2008). However, we believe that the cognitive and cognitive behavioural therapies would benefit immensely from putting emotion back in place – from putting the horse back in front of the cart, otherwise the cart is simply going to sit there and not go anywhere. Every cart needs its horse, just as every cognitive system needs its emotion. The horse drives the cart, and emotion drives the cognitive system. So we have labelled this approach to therapy as *Emotion-Focused Cognitive Therapy*, because whilst we are arguing for the importance of the horse, we also acknowledge the importance of the cart and do not want the horse to run off without it.

In the remainder of this introductory chapter therefore, we present, first, the standard approach to cognitive and cognitive behavioural therapy, especially in the approach originally developed by Aaron Beck (1976) and his colleagues (Beck et al., 1979). We consider both the strengths and weaknesses of this model, and then the next generation of cognitive behavioural models in which emotion was not merely considered to be the outcome of cognitive processing, but was considered to feed back into cognitive processes and thereby influence those processes: models such as John Teasdale's (1983) differential activation approach and its role in depression and David Clark's (1986) model of panic. These models made cognitive therapies more powerful and extended the range of problems to which cognitive therapies began to be applied. However, we believe that even these models are not powerful enough because they do not have an underlying theory of emotion, but simply take emotion as a given. In the final part of the chapter, our own model of emotion and cognition is presented, the SPAARS approach (in which the letters stand for different types of internal representation systems that we believe are involved in mental processes: Schematic Model, Propositional, Analogue, and Associative Representation Systems). The crucial difference between SPAARS as a multilevel system is that, in contrast to the earlier cognitive behavioural systems, there are two different routes to the generation of emotion and these routes can variously be congruent with each other or in conflict with each other. The consequences of the experience and regulation of emotion are thereby extended to the extent that we believe we need the subsequent chapters of this book to begin to spell them out. First, however, we need to set the scene through a consideration of the early standard cognitive behavioural model.

Early or 'Standard' Cognitive Behaviour Therapy

The early cognitive therapy model of depression presented in Figure 1.1 is based on Beck et al. (1979). The model assumes that early childhood experiences such as critical parents, emotional neglect and so on lead to the formation of underlying dysfunctional assumptions or schema of the type 'I must do everything well in order to be a good person' and 'Unless I am loved by everybody, I am worthless'. The model assumes that these schemas can remain dormant or latent for many years into adulthood or even older adulthood. However, they can be activated by a matching life event or difficulty that leads to the activation of the schema. For example, a young woman's first serious love affair as a teenager ends in disaster and leaves her feeling completely rejected. Her underlying assumption that she must be loved by everybody otherwise she is worthless is now activated and she becomes preoccupied with thoughts of being a worthless person. Such 'negative automatic thoughts', as Beck calls them, can appear automatically and out of the blue, and they lead to downturns in mood and subsequent depression. The crucial process for the development

Figure 1.1　The classic cognitive therapy model of depression

of depression within the early model is therefore the occurrence of these negative automatic thoughts (NATs) that lead to depression.

Beck initially developed his cognitive therapy approach as a short-term here-and-now focused treatment for depression. Much of the therapeutic focus in early cognitive therapy was therefore on the identification and subsequent challenging of these NATs. And for many practitioners, and neophyte cognitive therapists, the use of diary sheets on which to record NATs remains at the core of their therapeutic work. The problem however is that depression is far more complex than the swatting of NATs would have us believe, and many new therapists can eventually despair of the complex issues that can be lost behind a wall of diary sheets (i.e. if the diaries have been completed in the first place). Let us briefly consider a clinical example:

> Peter was a 33-year old dustman who had been referred by his GP following the break-up of his marriage. He had arrived home unexpectedly one day and found his wife together with the father of a schoolfriend of his daughter. He had walked out and vowed never to return. He felt overwhelmed by feelings of disgust and anger especially when he realised that his wife had been having sex with both him and her lover for some months. These realisations left Peter overwhelmed by *feelings* of shame, disgust, and humiliation.

As part of the initial therapeutic work with Peter, a three-column diary record, as shown in Figure 1.2, was implemented; thus, Peter was asked to record in the diary any difficult situation that he was in

Situation	Irrational thoughts	Feelings
Thursday – woke up early at 6 a.m. after bad dreams		Feeling shaky and sick and still very tired
Friday afternoon – in *Newsagents* and see picture of attractive woman in bikini on front of magazine		Hands start shaking and feel hot and sweaty
Saturday morning – lying in bed half awake		A feeling terribly lonely
Sunday morning – sitting in Church		Feeling lonely and embarrassed
Sunday afternoon – watching TV alone at home		An overwhelming feeling of fatigue

Figure 1.2 The three-column diary record for Peter

during the week, what thoughts occurred to him in that situation and what his feelings were. The first week he returned to therapy but with a blank diary sheet. He explained that because he knew how important the NATs were from the *Coping with Depression* booklet he had read the week before, he had not completed the diary sheet because he had no such thoughts. The basic principles of cognitive therapy were explained to Peter again, and again he went away fully determined to capture any NATS that came his way. The following week Peter returned to therapy with plenty written in his diary sheet apart from in the column 'Irrational Thoughts'. For example, he described waking up in the morning and instantly feeling overwhelmed with nausea, humiliation and anger but without having *thought* about anything first. These feelings seemed to be there as he awoke, and they did not appear to be triggered by NATs.

It is hard to know from the relevant literature how often cognitive therapists have patients like Peter whose emotions and moods do not appear to be triggered by reportable NATs. In fact, it would be a very useful and interesting piece if a young researcher took up the challenge and provided an answer for us. But whether the answer is that there are many or very few such NAT-free cases, the fact that a proportion of any cognitive therapist's caseload must consist of such cases raises the question of what therapists do when this happens. Perhaps the comment about Freudian patients that they always came to have Freudian dreams and Jungian patients came to have Jungian dreams might be applicable; perhaps, clients may be suggestible enough to begin to have NATs if you persist long enough pursuing them as a therapist – if the clients can stand such therapy for that long. Of course, we know from the work on false memories that the therapeutic encounter is an extremely powerful one and that some clients may even falsely recollect memories of abuse, alien abduction or such, if that is the line being pushed by the therapist (Power, 2002). So having a few negative thoughts is small fry compared to alien abduction or imagined abuse.

One of the responses of the cognitive therapy community has been an attempt to de-emphasize NATs and re-focus instead on the putative dysfunctional schemas that were meant to be driving the whole process. Jeff Young (1999) took this notion a step further and developed a *Schema-Focused Cognitive Therapy* in which the underlying schemas became the focus of therapy in place of the identifications and challenging of NATs. But there is no inherent reason why if NATs have failed to provide the whole story, should even bigger NATs (or should we call them BEES [Big Everything Encompassing Schemas) provide the whole story either? Again, there is no question that some clients will be helped by the identification and challenging of such underlying BEES, but then when these in turn fail to provide the whole story, cognitive therapists can chase even bigger nasties. In fact, Beck (1996) has taken this route with the suggestion in anxiety disorders of *Modes* (which, to continue the insect analogy, appear to be *swarms of BEES*). The point that we wish to make is that there are many strengths to the cognition-focused approach, but there may be many limitations because of the failure to give emotion its rightful place. Before however we look at modern multilevel theories of emotion, we will first consider a second generation of 'sophisticated' CBT models, in which the causal role of emotion is being increasingly emphasized.

'Sophisticated' Cognitive Therapy

The pioneering work of researchers such as John Teasdale (1983) and Gordon Bower (1981) began to open the cognitive behavioural world to the possibility that cognition and emotion (i.e. thinking and feeling) interact with each other; that sometimes feeling states make us more likely to think in a particular way, just as, in early cognitive therapy, thinking can lead us to feel in a particular way. Figure 1.3 expresses these ideas very simply: The initial cognitive therapy model considered a linear causal chain shown in Figure 1.3a in which cognition causes emotion, but subsequent work suggested that cognition and emotion may interact with each other rather than one take causal priority over the other (as shown in Figure 1.3b). So, for example, Gordon Bower (1981) demonstrated that if someone is in a sad mood they may be less likely to recall positive memories and more likely to think about negative memories. Some problems in replicating some of the detail of these early studies (see Power & Dalgleish, 2008) have been there; nevertheless, the work was important because it suggested possibilities for emotional disorders such as in depression and anxiety. What if, in vulnerable individuals, they are sometimes unable to protect themselves against certain types of thoughts or thinking once they enter a particular feeling state?

a)　PROBLEMS WITH STANDARD COGNITIVE THERAPY

(a)　**Cognition** ⎯⎯⎯⎯→ **Emotion**

b)　PROBLEMS WITH STANDARD COGNITIVE THERAPY

(b)　**Cognition**  **Emotion**

Figure 1.3　Cognition and emotion

In response to such developments, the cognitive therapy model of depression began to change along the lines shown in Figure 1.4. The earlier model (see Figure 1.1 earlier) was still incorporated into the new model, but now positive feedback loops were added that recognized the interplay between NATs, mood state, physiology and behaviour. A classic example in depression would be that as a person's mood deteriorates, he or she begins to withdraw from everyday activities and stay longer and longer in bed – mood and behavioural changes that would also lead to further physiological changes and to increased thoughts of personal inadequacy. One of the key therapeutic interventions with such inactive depression is therefore to break

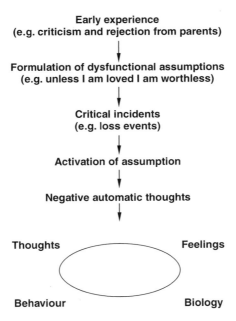

Figure 1.4 The revised cognitive therapy model of depression

into the vicious cycle that maintains the system shown in Figure 1.4 and keeps the person in a state of chronic depression. The use of graded tasks at which the person can achieve some success is an important method for breaking into this inactivity cycle in certain types of depression.

A second example of the introduction into cognitive behavioural therapies of cognition-emotion cycles is in David Clark's (1986) cognitive model of panic illustrated in Figure 1.5. The cognition-emotion cycle in this model is typically started with awareness of a physical change such as heart beating faster. If this physical change is interpreted in a catastrophic way, for example, 'I am having a heart attack,' then a vicious cycle commences that can lead to the experience of a full-blown panic attack. Clark and his colleagues have shown that a number of different types of panic attack can be accounted for in this way: physical constriction around the throat can lead to panic about suffocation; light-headedness can lead to panic about brain haemorrhaging and feelings of psychic anxiety can lead to feelings of loss of control and madness. Similar to the treatment of depression, the key to the treatment of panic attacks is to find an appropriate point

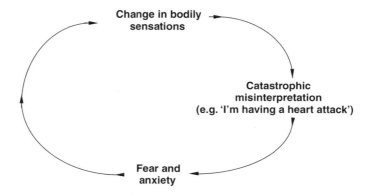

Figure 1.5   Clark's cognitive therapy model of panic

to intervene in the vicious cycle that is seen to cause the panic. As in the early cognitive therapy model, the preferred point is to attack the NAT, or the 'catastrophic misinterpretation' as it has been re-labelled, so perhaps we should now say attack the CAT (i.e. the catastrophic automatic thought).

There is no doubt that Clark's cognitive therapy for panic attacks has some success, and there are now randomized controlled trials that demonstrate its effectiveness, certainly when Clark and his colleagues carry out the treatment (Clark et al., 1994). However, the NAT problem, or the NAT-CAT problem as we should now call it, that we had raised for the early cognitive therapy model of depression still exists. Clark's model may be effective for the treatment of panic attacks with catastrophic misinterpretations, but many panic attacks are not preceded by conscious propositional statements such as 'I am having a heart attack'. The existence of such non-catastrophic-thought panic attacks means that the Clark model is of limited applicability, albeit useful for those panic attacks to which it does apply. Consider the following case example:

John was a 25-year old postgraduate student who was taking longer with writing his thesis than planned. His grant had finished some months before and he had run up debts in order to give himself time to complete his thesis before looking for paid work. Because of the pressure he was under, his relationship had recently finished and his girlfriend had moved out to live with someone else. In spite of all of these problems and pressures, John reported that he was working well, if perhaps too hard, and that he believed he would finish eventually and get his life back on track. The only problem was that for the past few weeks he had begun having night terrors in which he woke up sweating and shouting in absolute panic almost every night. He remembered having similar night terrors as a child and had been to see his GP and eventually the terrors had gone away. The theme of the current terrors was always similar, for example, he would start dreaming that he was being locked in a coffin and could not get out, or that he was being suffocated and could not breathe, or that he was trapped in a room or lift and no-one could hear his screams.

The night terror panic attacks John experienced were typically preceded by a nightmarish dream; however, on systematically recording their occurrence, not all of them were preceded by recallable dreams: sometimes he simply woke up in terror. The existence of night terrors and other similar panic phenomena that are not clearly preceded by negative thoughts again provides a challenge for the second generation of more sophisticated cognitive therapy models. We believe (Power & Dalgleish, 1997, 2008) that the problem is that the basic theory is wrong and that it is too simple. The cognitive therapies over-emphasize the role of thought in emotional disorders, and they lack an adequate theory of emotion, as we outline in the next section.

Dual Process Models in Psychology

We should not be too harsh on cognitive therapy and make it sound as if it suffers from fatal theoretical inadequacies when similar problems have been evident in other areas of psychology as well. Let us take the example of attitude and attitude change from the area of social psychology as a telling example (see Chaiken & Trope, 1999, for more detail). The majority of fair-minded individuals would like to think of themselves as free of prejudice and support non-racist, non-sexist and non-ageist views and policies; that is, their stated or *explicit* attitudes demonstrate how fair-minded and liberal they are. However, the truth tends to be less straightforward and more complex; when it comes to measures of behaviour, automatic perceptual processes, reaction time measures and psychophysiology, there may well be indicators of prejudice and bias which the individual would consciously reject (Chaiken & Trope, 1999). In other words, people's *implicit* attitudes may sometimes conflict with their explicit attitudes. Such a system that leads to conflicting attitudes occurring in parallel with each other *cannot* be readily accommodated in the cognitive therapy models that we have considered so far because the models do not allow for parallel processes that potentially conflict with each other and produce different outcomes.

There is of course a considerable history within other areas of psychology for the idea of processes running in parallel with each other that are potentially in conflict. Hermann von Helmholtz, the great German nineteenth-century scientist, had, long before Freud, argued for the need for unconscious or automatic processes in visual perception and demonstrated conditions under which apparently integrated processes disintegrated or produced errors such as in visual illusions (Power, 1997). The psychoanalytic approach developed by Freud includes preconscious, conscious and unconscious systems which are typically in conflict with each other and are often in conflict within themselves; thus, the unconscious system is not considered to hold information in a consistent and logical manner but contains contradictory and apparently illogical material (Freud, 1915). The model that we present does not owe its allegiance to psychoanalysis but is squarely based in modern cognitive approaches to emotion. Nevertheless, there are many insights within the psychoanalytic approach that inform both theory and practice in therapy, which we acknowledge as we proceed.

Our main point of departure from extant models in cognitive therapy, therefore, is in the need for two distinct sets of conscious and unconscious or automatic processes that sometimes act in synergy but at other times produce conflicting outputs. In addition to the evidence for two such routes or sets of processes that we have briefly cited from areas such as social cognition and psychoanalysis, there is also increasing evidence from research in neuroscience that two such separate routes exist. For example, Joseph LeDoux's (1996) work on the acquisition and maintenance of fear in rats clearly shows the need for a fast fear-based system that operates through the amygdala in the mid-brain (or what used to be known as the limbic system) and a higher route through the cortex. These two routes can operate in tandem and synergistically or can produce conflicting outputs depending on the exact conditions and circumstances. LeDoux's work in animals, together with similar work in human neuroscience, points to the need for more complex multilevel systems to understand emotion reactions in humans. In the next section therefore, we outline our own SPAARS model of emotion and demonstrate the need for more complex models that do justice to the phenomena under consideration and provide a richer basis for the therapeutic endeavours needed to work with a range of emotional disorders.

The SPAARS Approach

My colleague Tim Dalgleish and I have developed the SPAARS model over the past decade or so (Power & Dalgleish, 1997, 2008). Many illustrious and influential multilevel theories of emotion have been available before our model, in particular, the works of Howard Leventhal and Klaus Scherer (1987) and John Teasdale and Phil Barnard (1993). We hope that we have incorporated only the best aspects of these models into our own SPAARS approach and omitted some of the weaker aspects.

The SPAARS model is presented in Figure 1.6. The various types of representation and processing systems are as follows:

1. *The analogical system:* This system refers to a collection of primarily sensory-specific systems that include vision, hearing, taste, smell, touch and kinaesthetic systems. These sensory systems

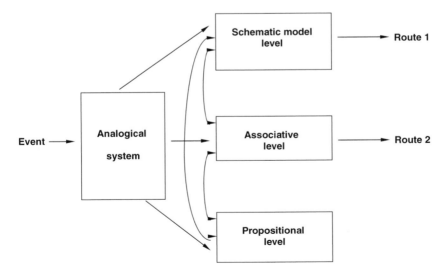

Figure 1.6 The SPAARS model

provide the initial processing of external events that are often emotion-provoking and for that reason often become directly incorporated into perception and memory of emotional events.

2. *The associative system:* This system typically operates automatically and outside awareness; it includes the innate-based starting points for the emotion and other systems that develop over time according to associative learning mechanisms; skills-based actions and repeated sequences also increase in their automaticity and become represented at this level so that frequently repeated appraisal emotion sequences can eventually occur automatically and outside awareness.

3. *The propositional system:* This system is the one beloved of cognitive therapy in which verbal–linguistic statements (propositions) are represented. However, in contrast to cognitive therapy we do not believe that propositions directly cause emotions, but propositions such as NATs and CATs must be further processed either through the associative system or through the schematic model system in order to generate emotion.

4. *The schematic model system:* This is the high-level system in which dynamic and ever-changing models of the self and the world are constructed and which provides overall executive control. In relation to emotion, effortful appraisal of events and situations leads to schematic models that generate emotions; appraisals typically evaluate events and situations in relation to key goals, both personal and interpersonal, with the appraisal outcomes generating different emotions.

These four proposed systems combine to produce two routes to emotion as illustrated in Figure 1.6 . A high-level effortful appraisal based route operates through the schematic model system, and a low-level typically automatic route occurs through the associative system. The operation of the two systems can be observed under various circumstances and for various emotions. A very simple example is the stepping-into-the-road reaction when a fleeting movement out of the corner of one's eye causes a sudden jump back as you orient towards whatever was apparently moving towards you; further slower attentional processing via the schematic model system confirms that indeed it was a bus moving rapidly towards you and the feeling of panic increases because of the near miss. Alternatively, full attentional processing reveals that it was just a leaf blowing in the wind so we laugh it off and make a joke about it to our companion. This simple example illustrates one of the functions of the automatic associative system – the immediate interruption of current activity when the organism may have come under sudden and unexpected threat, which the slower schematic model system provides more detailed and elaborative processing of so that emotion and action become synergistic.

Later chapters in this book are replete with examples of how the two routes can be in conflict with each other, but it is still useful to illustrate this point at this stage with a relatively common and persuasive example. Individuals who suffer from simple phobias (see Chapter 5) can often report conflicting experiences about the phobic object as in the following example:

> Jane was a nurse who had worked in hospitals all her adult life, but her job was just about to change and she was being moved into the community. She was referred for help because she was on the verge of giving up her career because she was terrified that she would come across dogs in the community, including when visiting people in their homes if they owned dogs and she would not be able to enter their homes. She had experienced a phobia of dogs from a very young age, as had her mother, though on assessment she was unable to recall any traumatic or other negative experiences with dogs. In fact, when she thought carefully about dogs, she understood that people could be very fond of them and even have dogs as their best friends. The problem was however that she began to panic if ever she saw a dog, especially if one unexpectedly ran towards her or jumped up at her.

Jane's mixed reaction is not uncommon amongst those with simple animal phobias: on the one hand, she reacted with panic if ever a dog was near her (i.e. emotion generated via the associative route), on the other, when she thought carefully about dogs she could feel mildly positive about them and certainly understand other people's strongly positive reactions to dogs (i.e. effortful appraisal occurring via the schematic model route leading to a mildly positive reaction). Many individuals with animal and other simple phobias often report that they know that their fears are 'irrational' (a schematic model appraisal), but they are unable to do anything about their fear or panic because it is automatically generated via associative route mechanisms. Such fears and phobias provide dramatic examples of how the two routes to emotion generation can provide different and even conflicting outcomes ('I love you, but I also hate you!'). But we leave further discussion of such examples to later chapters in the book in the context of assessment (Chapter 3) and therapy (Chapter 4 onwards).

In the next chapter, however, we take a necessary diversion to consider the question of 'What Is an Emotion?' One of the problems with the cognitive behavioural therapies, and other recent therapies designed to tackle the emotional disorders (e.g. interpersonal psychotherapy and many humanistic therapies), is that they do not have a theory of emotion. Emotions are simply 'givens', which typically means a list of emotions based either on folk psychology or on the theoretically empty classification systems such as the *American Diagnostic and Statistical Manual* system (currently *DSM-IV*, American Psychiatric Association, 1994). This approach to emotion leads to an absurd arbitrariness that swings around with fashion; thus, if an eminent psychiatrist persuades the *DSM-V* taskforce (which is currently meeting) that 'schadenfreude' is a serious emotional disorder that needs to be included in the next classification system, then somewhere in California a psychotherapy will be invented called schadenfreude therapy (most likely to be shortened to 'SCHAT') and before we know it, people all around the world will be being SCHAT-upon to treat their excess schadenfreude. There is one good way out of this mess, and that is to get a decent theory of emotion! Of course, we have given away our punchline – we think the SPAARS approach *is* a decent theory of emotion. But we do not want therapists to have to take this assertion on the grounds of faith alone. First, we need to review what has happened in the whole area of emotion so that readers too might come to the conclusion that the current multilevel theories of emotion are the best we have at present and, just as importantly, that they provide potential clinical therapeutic insights that have only just begun to be realized.

2
What is an Emotion?

In the classic film *The Invasion of the Body Snatchers*, Don Siegal portrayed humanoid species that were not detectably different from humans except eventually through one feature – they lacked emotions (Power & Dalgleish, 1997). The film is an enduring classic that has been remade several times including the most recent version *The Invasion* starring Nicole Kidman. When asked, some people respond that they have a boss or a neighbour who has clearly suffered the same fate, but the absence or near absence of emotion in such cases (see Chapter 6) is cause for concern rather than envy. The point is that emotions are inextricably part of being human and creatures or machines without emotion are like the Mr Spocks of the world, and we feel sorry for them even if we can sometimes be amused by them.

The modern view, as these brief examples testify to, is that emotions are *functional* in our lives, but too much or too little of any of these can be a problem. Unfortunately, this functional approach to emotion has been out of fashion in much of Western culture for at least 2,000 years (Oatley, 2005). Many of our ambivalent attitudes to emotion and the view that somehow reason and emotion are opposed to each other stem from this long history. A catalogue of famous philosophers and scientists viewed emotions as anything but functional; Darwin saw emotions as vestigial remnants of our evolutionary past, and the only people free of them were Victorian males such as he, who were at the top of the evolutionary tree. The following quote from Plato sums up this approach nicely:

> In men the organ of generation – becoming rebellious and masterful, like an animal disobedient to reason, and maddened with the sting of lust – seeks to gain absolute sway; and the same is the case with the . . . womb . . . of women; the animal within them is desirous of procreating children, and when remaining unfruitful long beyond its proper time, gets discontented and angry, and wandering in every direction through the body, closes up the passages of the breath, and by obstructing respiration, drives them to extremity, causing all varieties of diseases. (Plato, 1957)
>   Reproduced from Plato (1953). *The Timaeus* [B. Jowett trans]
>   Oxford University Press.

In this statement, Plato not only pitches reason against the animal passions for both men and women but also introduces the 'wandering uterus' disorder for women, which subsequently came to be known as 'hysteria'. We now know that hysteria is not a result of a wandering or dissatisfied uterus and that it can be experienced by men and women. More serious though is the view still prevalent in our society that emotions are bad, that they undermine reason and that their presence is indicative of disorder.

Plato therefore has much to answer for – in addition to his legacy in the view that we should rid ourselves of all of emotions and rely solely on reason, he contributed significantly to the 'genderization' of emotions in our culture. We began viewing certain emotions such as fear and sadness as 'weak and feminine' and emotions such as anger as 'strong and masculine'. These views of emotion become dysfunctionally exaggerated in many clinical presentations, as numerous examples throughout this book suggest.

To set the scene for the rest of this chapter in which we ask 'What Is an Emotion?', we start with an attempted, if lengthy, definition of emotion. At least some aspects of the definition are controversial, but these are picked up and dealt with in detail in subsequent sections of the chapter:

> Emotions are mental and bodily states that typically comprise a constellation of physiological, behavioural and psychological processes that follow the appraisal or evaluation of a situation or event as relevant to the individual's goals. These goals range from basic drive-based survival goals to higher-order interpersonal and aesthetic goals. There are a limited set of such emotion states that include fear, sadness, anger disgust and happiness, all of which have come to signal in a multitask multilevel

system shifts in the priority of goal-based functioning and from which an infinite range of more complex emotions are derivable. These emotion states are normally short-lived in nature and need only last a matter of seconds or minutes; when they become more chronic, they are normally referred to as 'moods' for which the instigating situation or event may have been forgotten. The conscious aspect of an emotion is referred to as its 'affect' or 'feeling', though under many circumstances emotions can be unconscious and have no reportable affect state.

This definition of emotion offers a working approach that we believe will help to inform the clinical endeavours detailed throughout this book. However, it is worth noting at least some of the more controversial issues included in the definition, such as the following:

1. The distinction between 'mental' and 'physical' states: This distinction is used here in a pragmatic way and does not imply any Cartesian mind–body dualism or a split between body and mind. Indeed, the beauty of emotions is in that they provide the integrating force between our own attempted splits between mind and body. However, these splits are not of the Cartesian philosophical variety but of a psychopathological kind that can become a necessary focus in therapy.
2. The concept of 'appraisal': Many approaches to understanding the generation of emotions can largely be traced back to the 'feeling theories' of Plato and the functionalist theory of Aristotle espoused here. Functionalist theories have assumed that not the events in themselves but how these are evaluated according to personally relevant criteria is what is important. Modern cognitive approaches to emotion, as we show in detail later, are mostly appraisal based (Power & Dalgleish, 2008).
3. A goal-based definition: We believe that a crucial feature of events and situations is how they impact our goals and plans and that different emotions result from different types of impact. As noted earlier, these include survival goals, interpersonal and shared goals and aesthetic goals. Although emotions arising from mnemonic processes might superficially appear to run counter to this goal-based approach, the content of memory is normally about something that impacted relevant goals and plans in the past. Similarly, emotions arising from imaginative processes ('They would miss me if I weren't here!') typically involve events that would have an impact on goals and plans if they occurred in the future.

4. The proposal for 'basic emotions': The next section examines some of the arguments for and against dimensional approaches to emotion and to basic emotion categorical approaches. We (Power & Dalgleish, 2008) believe that both approaches have merits and that they are perhaps not as opposite to each other as sometimes presented. For example, we argue that the starting point for the associative system is a set of five basic emotions, whilst at the same time we acknowledge that conscious affect can be described along such dimensions as positive–negative, pleasant–unpleasant or calm–aroused. In a multilevel system such as SPAARS, different levels may operate on different principles. Perhaps more difficult to reconcile is, as we see, exactly how many basic emotions there are, given that previous commentators have failed to agree on this issue.

5. Conscious versus unconscious emotions: There is nothing like the notion of the unconscious to divide opinion! Despite working together for many years on emotion and on the SPAARS approach, my colleague Tim Dalgleish and I have simply agreed to disagree on the concept of 'unconscious emotion', a topic that divides the whole community of emotion researchers fairly equally (see Ekman & Davidson, 1994). Researchers such as my colleague Tim argue that for emotion proper to occur, there has to be a conscious experience of affect, otherwise a reaction without such conscious affect is not a full emotion (though what it is instead, I am not quite clear – perhaps it should be called a 'motion', which is perhaps what is left following their viewpoint if you drop the 'e' for 'experience' from 'emotion'). Interestingly, even Freud (1915) argued that there has to be conscious affect for something to be labelled an emotion:

> It is surely of the essence of an emotion that we should feel it, i.e. that it should enter consciousness. So for emotions, feelings and affects to be unconscious would be quite out of the question' (p. 104).

However, according to me, the SPAARS model (see Chapter 1 for a summary) necessitates that we call the outcome of the direct associative route to emotion 'unconscious emotions', because the associative route can generate without conscious awareness. Numerous studies of psychophysiology, subliminal perception and dissociative phenomena demonstrate the existence of emotion-type effects without conscious awareness, and the most parsimonious approach seems to be to call such states emotions. We of course return to this dispute at various points throughout the book.

Emotion: Dimensions Versus Categories

The issue of whether emotions are best represented by dimensions such as valence and arousal or are best thought of as discrete entities or categories has generated considerable debate and led to divisions in the recent past (Ekman, 1992; Russell, 1994). A strong tradition since the work at least of Osgood in the 1950s (Osgood et al., 1957) has shown that analyses of a range of emotion terms and of emotion experiences typically based on self-report measures of affect such as the Positive and Negative Affect Scale (PANAS) (Watson et al., 1988) highlight the importance of two key dimensions along which specific emotion terms can be located.

As shown in Figures 2.1 and 2.2, two different approaches have emerged within the dimensional tradition. In the first view, theorists such as Russell and Carroll (1999) argue that the positive and negative

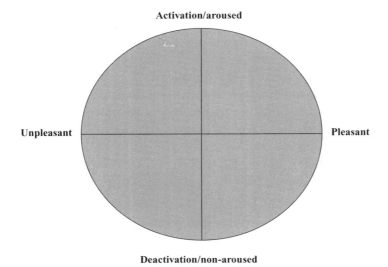

Figure 2.1   Russell's dimensional approach to affect

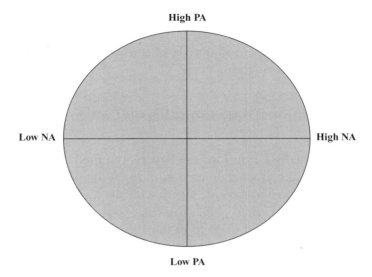

Figure 2.2 Watson and Clark's dimensional approach to affect. PA, positive affectivity; NA, negative affectivity

form bipolar opposites at the ends of one dimension, whereas arousal forms the other dimension (see Figure 2.1). In contrast, researchers such as Watson and Clark (1992) have argued that the positive and the negative dimensions are orthogonal to each other so that some emotional states can be high on both positive and negative dimensions (e.g. some types of anger or disruptive forms of elation), a property that would be missed if the positive and negative are seen as opposites on the same bipolar dimension.

These dimensional approaches to emotion are located within a productive approach within psychology in which equivalent or conceptually related ideas have been presented in areas adjoining or even overlapping with emotion research. For example, Rolls (1999) has developed earlier notions of approach and avoidance into important motivational systems, similar to the earlier work on the behavioural activation and behavioural inhibition systems developed by Jeffrey Gray (1982). Davidson (2000) has also argued along similar lines on the basis of recent neurophysiological scanning data that valence and arousal are important aspects of emotion processing in the brain.

OK, so let us say that there exists considerable evidence that brain processes can respond to the types of albeit simplistic dimensions that a range of researchers have posited over the years. From the area of emotion and adjoining areas such as motivation and learning, these dimensions are typically based on principles such as approach avoidance and positive–negative valence. However, does the existence of and evidence for such dimensions imply that the brain does not therefore operate on other principles as well? Well, the answer from modern multilevel approaches to emotion is that different levels may operate using different principles. For example, schematic models of conscious affect might readily incorporate issues of valence and approach-avoidance because they are important appraisal components for the evaluation of events and situations (though one would predict important individual differences in the extent to which different individuals incorporated such information, even if overall group statistics showed general effects for valence and approach avoidance). In contrast, the analogical and associative systems might provide stronger evidence for innate-based basic emotion systems. And although the two systems must overlap with each other, one of the important functions of a multilevel system is that the 'evolutionary shortcuts' that a single-level system might offer can be overridden in a more complex system.

Take the example of anxiety. In a single-level approach-avoidance positive–negative system, anxiety would be an emotion associated with avoidance. In many situations, such avoidance anxiety is right, and it helps us avoid dangerous animals, dangerous heights, people armed with weapons, or such. However, there are situations in which both anxiety and the need to approach rather than avoid exist; for example, to go on stage and receive the school prize – the teenager may feel both highly anxious and highly motivated to approach the feared situation. And such approach anxiety blends into excitement in many fairground and other situations. The problem for a single-level system is that it suddenly needs to become more complex in that it needs to generate numerous exceptions to its simplistic rules of the relationship between straightforward emotions such as anger, anxiety, sadness and disgust and the dimensions of positive–negative and approach-avoidance. The SPAARS answer to these problems is to argue that the different levels may incorporate different principles into their operation (Power & Dalgleish, 2008), as we explore in detail when we consider the basic emotions approach in the next section.

Basic Emotions

The world's leading emotion researcher, Paul Ekman, tells a very interesting story of how he became convinced that there are a set of basic emotions that are universally recognisable in all cultures. As a young researcher, Ekman (2003) tells how, like most others in anthropology and psychology in the 1960s, he assumed that emotions and emotion expression were primarily culture specific and dismissed Darwin's (1872) suggestion that there might be universals in emotion and facial expression to an extent that:

> I was so convinced that he [Darwin] was wrong that I didn't bother to read his book (Ekman, 2003, p. 2).

Ekman (2003) serendipitously received money to test the universality versus culture specific hypothesis among a range of cultures, including the Fore in the Highlands of Papua and New Guinea, who had been completely protected from the modern world and had no television, photography or written language. Again, Ekman is worth quoting directly:

> Are expressions universal, or are they, like language, specific to each culture? Irresistible! I really didn't care who proved to be correct, although I didn't think it would be [universality]. . . . I found just the opposite of what I thought I would discover' (p. 3).

To cut a long though still-continuing story short, Ekman found both to his and to other researchers' surprise evidence for the universality of facial expression of emotion across a wide range of cultures.

Over the subsequent years, Ekman has at different times proposed different lists of basic emotions, initially considering fear, anger, surprise, disgust, happiness and sadness, but then adding contempt, and more recently dividing happiness into sensory pleasure (which Ekman suggests could be five emotions rather than one), amusement, contentment, excitement, relief, wonderment, ecstasy, fiero (a type of pride), naches (another type of pride), elevation, gratitude and schadenfreude (Ekman, 2003). These developments illustrate both the great strengths of Ekman's approach and the fatal flaws in his approach to emotion. Ekman has primarily based his approach to emotion on a single system, the face, with occasional dips into peripheral psychophysiology. Unfortunately, at no point has he ever presented a full definition of emotion, otherwise sensory pleasures such as the taste of food would not be categorized as an emotion; emotions such as contempt would be analysed as complex rather than basic emotions (Power & Dalgleish, 2008) and reactions such as surprise and startle would be seen as part of an orienting response but not as emotions in themselves. Part of the problem is that Ekman rejects appraisal as a necessary feature of emotion; thus, in his inclusion of sensory pleasures as emotions, he argues explicitly that these happen too fast for appraisal processes; therefore, appraisal cannot be an essential part of emotion. But hang on a minute! That sounds like the wrong way round to us; what if appraisal processes are precisely what differentiates emotion from non-emotion states? Moreover, what if appraisal processes can also become fast and automated if, for example, there are oft-repeated sequences? For example, what if every time a child cried or was miserable his mother gave him chocolate to cheer him up? The taste of chocolate may then come to be appraised in an emotionally positive way, though this appraisal process may become fast and automatic. However, the crucial distinction here is that a particular taste comes to generate emotion automatically via the associative route in SPAARS, but only this particular taste has such an emotional effect, whereas other tastes, despite occurring very rapidly, still would not have an inherent emotional evaluation.

To understand some of the problems that have arisen in emotion theory and research, we suggest therefore that too many researchers, even eminent ones, have over-focused on one system at the expense of other systems. Whilst Ekman has over-focused on facial expression, researchers such as Davidson and Russell, considered under the dimensional approaches earlier, have over-focused on conscious affect. However, the emotion system is based on multiple systems that have functions other than just the processing or the expression of emotion. For example, the face has multiple social expressive and communication functions that do not only involve emotion – expressions of welcome, surprise, startle, understanding, puzzlement or such; conscious affect is experienced in relation to a whole variety of events, situations and internal and external systems – pain, hunger, thirst, sexual excitement and temperature are just a few examples of the many affects and blends of affects that can occur but are not inherently emotional. To help us through this labyrinth, let us return to the guiding thread that we believe the SPAARS model offers in relation to basic emotions and their number and function.

SPAARS and Basic Emotions

The basic emotions that have been most widely agreed upon and included in almost all modern lists of basic emotions are the five shown in Table 2.1. Almost all commentators would agree that the emotions of anger, sadness, fear, disgust and happiness are 'basic' according to a range of criteria, though we have drawn the list from the seminal work of Oatley and Johnson-Laird (1987). Ekman (1999) has done most to summarize what the criteria of 'basicness' are, and these include the universality of the emotion, its association with specific signals (e.g. particular facial expressions), its presumed innateness, its early appearance during child development, its fast and automatic generation and a typically fast pattern of recovery. These characteristics of course begin to change during development with the pressures of culture and family that shape the regulation and expression of different emotions according to 'display rules'. In addition, more complex emotions develop with time, some of which may be unique to a culture, but with the starting point being one of the basic emotions from which they are therefore derivable (Johnson-Laird & Oatley, 1989).

We have argued elsewhere (see Power & Dalgleish, 1997, 2008) that the essential defining aspect that differentiates one emotion from another is its core appraisal, and we have offered a set of core appraisals in Table 2.1. These core appraisals are based on a set of relevant goals and plans for the individual. Let us consider briefly each of the five basic emotions. Each appraisal refers to a goal-based juncture at

Table 2.1   Appraisals for five basic emotions

Basic emotion	*Appraisal*
Sadness	Loss or failure (actual or possible) of valued role or goal
Happiness	Successful move towards or completion of a valued role or goal
Anger	Blocking or frustration of a role or goal through perceived agent
Fear	Physical or social threat to self or valued role or goal
Disgust	A person, object or idea repulsive to the self, and to valued roles and goals

Source: Power and Dalgleish (2008).

which the goals are personally relevant, whether in an immediate and direct manner or in a more indirect and abstract way.

Sadness is a consequence of the appraisal that there is an actual loss, or a possible loss of a valued role or goal; thus, losses of key significant others involve the loss of that relationship together with a whole range of subsidiary goals and plans entailed in key relationships. Equally, sadness could result from the loss of a favourite pen, or the memory of the loss of childhood, or the imagined loss of our job, or that someone important to us such as a child or our favourite team failed to achieve something we had hoped for. The losses therefore can be real or imagined, they can affect us directly or indirectly because they happen to other people that are important to us, and they can be recalled from our own past, or be experienced empathically when losses happen in a film or a novel to someone that we have identified with.

In contrast to sadness, *happiness* refers to the appraisal of movement towards or completion of a valued role or goal. In this definition, we restrict 'happiness' to brief states such as joy or elation rather than the state of 'life satisfaction' or Aristotle's notion of *eudaimonea* to which the highly overworked English word 'happiness' also refers. These brief states of happiness occur when we complete something, or win something, or do a good day's work, or get to meet someone we like, or our child does well in her homework, or our football team win a game, or the right person gets voted in as prime minister, or we recall a success that we had at school. At this point, it is worth returning briefly to Ekman's (2003) confusion about positive emotion states in his claim that states such as amusement, gratitude and schadenfreude should also be given the status of basic emotions. We would dispute such an approach and argue that each of these emotions is derivable from the basic emotion of happiness, as we have defined it here, as follows. *Amusement* is typically an aesthetic emotion, the equivalent of sadness or fear experienced at the movies – so let us use this as an excuse to tell a risqué joke and see why it (hopefully) evokes (some) amusement:

A young woman was sitting on a very crowded bus when a frail old lady got on and stood right in front of her. The young woman however didn't stand up to offer the old woman a seat, even though it was normal and expected to do so. Eventually the old woman said to her 'I am sorry, my dear, but would you mind giving me your seat, because I am too old to stand up?' 'Oh, I am so sorry,' replies the young woman, 'but you see I am pregnant and I have been told I should not exert myself so I need to stay sitting down.' 'My dear, I really do apologise. I had no idea you were pregnant, because, you know, it really doesn't show.' 'No,' comes the reply 'you are right! It really doesn't show after two hours, does it!

An amusing story typically creates a hypothetical scenario with a set of expectations that are not fulfilled because of an unexpected reason. In the story quoted, an expected action does not occur (the old woman is not offered the seat) for an unexpected but joyful reason (the young woman is allegedly pregnant), though the apparently joyful reason has again an unexpected element to it because it refers to a wished-for goal rather than one that has actually been achieved. Of course, one should not labour over such analyses of humour, but the indirect or empathic involvement in such fictional scenarios provides a whole range of brief emotion states that makers of soap operas rely on for success.

The third basic emotion that we consider in Table 2.1 is *anger*. The key appraisal that we and others have proposed for the generation of anger is the blocking of a goal, plan or role through a perceived agent. For example, you are at work and are behind with a grant application deadline, you go to the photocopier and there are two people there chatting away and in no hurry to finish with the photocopier. You feel your irritation increasing and eventually feel quite angry. By their actions, they are blocking the completion of a goal, and though unaware of your goal, by their agency, they are preventing your goal completion. This example highlights why even *inanimate* objects can be appraised as agents who are deliberately blocking your goal completion. The next time you go to the photocopier with only minutes to the grant application deadline, you find that the photocopier is broken and you kick out at it in anger and frustration. We *know* that inanimate objects like photocopiers, computers and that cupboard at home that will never open properly all deliberately set out to make our lives problematic!

At this point, it is also worth noting some issues raised by the earlier *non-appraisal* theories of anger. One of the most influential of these theories has been Leonard Berkowitz's (1999) frustration–aggression hypothesis. Berkowitz has argued that there are numerous drives or states that make people more aggressive; for example, if people are too hot, if they are in pain, if they are thirsty or in some other state of discomfort, Berkowitz and others have amassed a considerable body of evidence to show that anger, frustration, and aggression are much more likely to occur. However, as DiGiuseppe and Tafrate (2007) have recently argued, this body of data can also be taken as evidence for the automatic route to emotion generation within the SPAARS model. Similar to getting angry with photocopiers and with recalcitrant cupboards, we can get angry with states of the personal environment (too hot, too windy, etc.) and states of our bodies (too hot, too sweaty, etc.) too. There is no question that such reactions can occur without deliberate conscious appraisal via the automatic route, but even here these reactions are modifiable because of conscious appraisals; for example, if you have paid thousands of dollars to travel to a hot beach for your summer vacation, you are more likely to feel pleasure whilst lying on the beach feeling hot and sweaty rather than feeling angry and frustrated – the context and meaning of the situation is crucially important, not simply the temperature of the body.

Fear or *anxiety* is the next basic emotion. . The primary level at which fear is generated is at the appraisal of *physical* threat to the body; thus, the bear charging at you through the woods makes you so terrified that you climb a tree faster than you ever thought you could. Unfortunately though, it turns out to be the rare species of tree-climbing bear that was chasing you. Alternatively, your boss has asked to see you. You know that you have been underperforming at work, and rumours have been rife that the company has not been doing well and that cuts are going to be made. In this case, your *physical* self is not in any direct danger, but your *social* self and valued work roles and goals are under threat. The night before your meeting, you cannot sleep at all because of anxiety about the meeting with your boss in the morning. In the third example of anxiety, someone important to you rather than you yourself is the source of the anxiety. Your child has just been taken into hospital for emergency investigations because of abdominal pains of unknown origin. You feel so anxious and worried that you are unable to work or think about anything else other than your son's well-being and what the outcome might be. In fact, this example relates to recent classifications of the aetiological trauma for the development of posttraumatic stress disorder (PTSD); thus, *DSM-IV* (1994) includes traumatic events that happen to people who are significant to us – parents, partners and children – not just traumatic events that happen to ourselves.

These examples of the appraisal of anxiety all share threat to something that is important or valuable to us – be it our physical existence, our social standing or key relationships. The function of anxiety in these different circumstances is to motivate us to change something to protect what is valuable to us. These protective or defensive actions can be of the matter of milliseconds as we jump away from the speeding car, or they can be of a much more long-term nature when we give our children vitamin supplements because we are worried about their future health, or when we switch to unleaded petrol because of our worries about the environment.

The final basic emotion listed in Table 2.1 is that of *disgust*. The origins of disgust in food-based and body product reactions have been commented on since at least the time of Darwin (Rozin & Fallon, 1987). This primarily food focus led some earlier theorists to define the key appraisal for disgust around gustatory goals (Oatley & Johnson-Laird, 1987), but we have argued against this narrow view of the emotion of disgust, given that even in relation to body products there are many non-food related products that can evoke disgust including phlegm and sexual body products (Power & Dalgleish, 2008). Interestingly, the only body products that do not seem to evoke disgust are tears, which is probably because tears are uniquely human in that no other animal sheds tears as part of emotion expression; therefore tears are perceived as the least 'animal-like' of all body products (Power, 1999). Whilst we acknowledge the importance of disgust in food and food waste products, we nevertheless prefer to consider the relevant appraisal in terms of a more general repulsion towards any object, person or idea that is seen as distasteful to the self and to significant others.

The disgust-based reactions seen in some of the eating disorders in which both food or certain foodstuffs and aspects of body shape and size become repulsive seem relatively straightforward enough not to discuss at this point; we return to these disorders in later chapters. Perhaps less obvious is the role that we have suggested that disgust plays in depression, and in some types of phobias, obsessive–compulsive disorders (OCD), and PTSD. In all of these examples, there is some aspect of the self or the world that is seen as unwanted and contaminating; thus in OCD certain aspects of the world may be seen as dirty or contaminating, whereas in depression part of the self becomes unwanted and loathsome, and that the person tries to get rid of. We consider these examples in detail later in the book.

In summary, we believe that these five basic emotions provide the building blocks for our emotional lives and therefore for the full range of emotional disorders that are encountered. Before looking at these disorders in detail, it is, however, necessary to consider two further aspects of this approach to emotion. First is the idea that all other emotions are derived from one or more basic emotions. Second is the related proposal that emotions can become 'coupled' with each other in ways that can be detrimental and form the basis of some of the emotional disorders.

Complex Emotions

One of the central tenets of the basic emotions approach is that all complex emotions are derived from the set of five basic emotions. These derivations can either occur through additional cognitive elaboration of an emotion, through the blending of different emotions or through the process of coupling mentioned earlier. Examples of cognitive elaboration shown in Table 2.2 would include worry as an

Table 2.2 Examples of complex emotions derived from basic emotions

Basic emotion	Examples of complex emotions
Fear	Embarrassment (1)
	Worry
Sadness	Grief
Anger	Envy
	Jealousy
	Contempt
Happiness	Joy
	Love
	Nostalgia
Disgust	Guilt
	Shame
	Embarrassment (2)

Source: Power and Dalgleish (2008).
Note: Numbers in parentheses indicate different types of embarrassment.

elaboration of fear in which there is rumination about the future, and guilt as a form of disgust that is directed towards an action carried out by the self. Examples of emotion blends include contempt and nostalgia; thus, contempt, although listed under anger in Table 2.2, typically includes a measure of disgust combined with anger directed towards the person or object of contempt. Similarly, nostalgia, although listed under happiness, also includes a measure of sadness directed towards the person or situation that is the object of the nostalgia. Table 2.2 also illustrates another feature of the complexity of emotions, which is that the same emotion term in everyday usage can come to represent different emotion states; thus, the Table illustrates the case of embarrassment, one form of which is primarily derived from fear (e.g. a negative social evaluation anxiety), the second of which is derivable from disgust (e.g. a mild version of shame), and at least one further version (not shown) which is a positive version (e.g. when being complimented in public). Another example of the multiple uses of the same word in everyday language is the word 'disgust', which in addition to referring to a state of repulsion is also used to refer to being angry as in 'I am disgusted with you for turning up late' (Power, 2006). The third category, that of coupling, follows along similar lines to the ideas of cognitive elaboration and blending, but we consider it separately in the next section because of its putative role in psychopathology.

The other feature that should be noted about this approach to basic and derived complex emotions can be illustrated by analogy to language. Language is also based on a limited number of symbols such as letters, words or ideographs, but from this limited number an infinite number of different combinations can be generated. Similarly, a limited number of primary colours can be combined to give an infinite number of hues, tones and blends. So, although five might not sound like a large number to begin with, once you have allowed for the range of subtle personal, interpersonal and cultural elaborations and the infinite number of potential blends of two or more basic emotions, then the emotion system has the potential to generate a myriad of unique as well as universal emotion states. Without doubt historically and cross-culturally certain unique emotions have been apparent; classic examples of these unique emotions include the medieval state of 'awe', a religious emotion felt in the presence of god and the state of 'accidie', which was experienced as a type of spiritual fatigue (Harre, 1987; Oatley, 2005). A range of 'culture-bound syndromes' also clearly incorporate some unique emotion and belief states. For example, *koro* is a culture-specific condition in which Filipino men feel that their penises have retracted into their body; this is typically accompanied by much anxiety and distress.

Emotion Coupling

One of the proposals that we made while developing the SPAARS approach to emotion was that certain emotion modules might become 'coupled' with each other in ways that might lead to psychopathology (Power & Dalgleish, 1997, 2008). One or two related ideas have been noted in the psychopathology literature, such as in the influential ideas of 'fear of fear' (Goldstein & Chambless, 1978) and similar ideas about 'depression about depression'. The 'fear of fear' idea is especially relevant to understand how someone who has experienced an extremely aversive state such as a panic attack might go to considerable efforts to avoid such an experience in the future; that is, they might successfully avoid having another panic attack through continued avoidance but nevertheless live in a state of anxiety. We believe that similar couplings occur not just within emotion categories such as in these examples but between other emotion categories also and that these couplings are often linked to psychopathology as shown in Table 2.3.

Examples of 'coupled' emotions shown in Table 2.3 include happiness–anxiety and happiness–anger sometimes seen in manic states; anxiety–disgust seen in some phobias, OCDs, and types of PTSD; sadness–disgust seen in depression; and sadness–anger seen in grief (see Power & Dalgleish, 2008). Each of the examples in any individual case is more complex than merely consisting of coupling, as will be shown with case studies in later chapters. Nevertheless, these provide examples of different types of coupling mechanisms. For example, in PTSD the victim may evaluate his experience of anxiety in a rejecting self-disgust fashion, which can happen to some male victims of assaults who had seen themselves as tough and invulnerable before the assault; for example, following their feelings of panic and anxiety, they now appraise themselves as weak and pathetic, which leads to feelings of self-disgust as well as anxiety. In this PTSD example, the coupling is caused by the appraisal of one emotion as weak and

Table 2.3 Basic emotions and emotional disorders

Basic emotion	Coupled emotion	Emotional 'disorder'
Fear	–	Panic
	–	Phobias (1)
	–	OCD (1)
	–	GAD
	–	PTSD (1)
	Disgust	PTSD (2)
Sadness	Anger	Pathological grief
	Disgust	Depression
Anger		Pathological anger
		Morbid jealousy
Happiness		Pollyannaism/pathological optimism
		Hypomania/mania
		Love sickness
		De Clérambault's syndrome
Disgust	? Fear	Phobias (2)
	?Fear	OCD (2)
		Suicide
		Eating disorders, etc.

Note: Numbers in parentheses indicate different types of each disorder. '?' indicate the possibility of fear.
OCD, obsessive compulsive disorder; GAD, generalized anxiety disorder; PTSD, posttraumatic stress disorder.

unacceptable, thereby leading to a second emotion. Again, in depression the coupling of self-disgust can occur directly with sadness, especially in some male depressions, but self-disgust is more typically directed at the self in addition to any other specific emotion; for example, following the break-up of a romantic relationship a woman might feel sad because of the loss and also anxious about surviving alone, whilst at the same time despising herself for needing a relationship and not being completely self-sufficient. In such cases, the coupling may be both direct and indirect in that it is more the cause of the sadness (that of needing a relationship) than perhaps the sadness itself that becomes the focus of the self-disgust (Power & Tarsia, 2007).

The proposal for the coupling of emotions as suggested in the SPAARS model has primarily been supported by clinical and anecdotal evidence. Recently, however, one of my PhD students, John Fox, tested a group of bulimic students in a priming paradigm to assess the prediction that anger and disgust could be coupled in bulimia. A group of female students who met clinical criteria for bulimia as well as a matched control group of healthy controls were given an anger induction task. Their levels of anger and disgust were tested immediately before and after the task. The results showed that both groups showed similar levels of disgust and anger before the priming procedure and that afterwards both showed significant increases in anger (though somewhat more in the bulimia group); most interesting, however, was the finding of a significant increase in the disgust levels in the bulimia group but no change in disgust levels in the control group (Fox & Harrison, 2008). Although in need of replication and extension, these results show some support for the proposed coupling of anger and disgust in bulimia (see Chapter 7 for a detailed background information about this link) and also how the priming methodology can be used to test predicted couplings in other disorders, in addition to the self-report methods that we have also used (Power & Tarsia, 2007).

Summary and Conclusions

This chapter has provided a very quick tour of the continent of emotion. Some theorists say that this continent can best be described as two dimensions, which, to continue with the geographical analogy, are the equivalent of how low or high the ground is above sea level and how soft or hard the terrain is. Although these descriptors are informative, we believe that to understand the continent of emotion fully, one must understand plate tectonics, that is, the interactions between the five underlying plates whose forces create the different heights and depths and many other properties of the emotion continent. These five basic emotions, we suggest, provide the basis for our entire emotional life in a way that complex emotions are derivable from one or more of the five emotions and that this is also true for the emotional disorders. However, before we go on to consider these emotional disorders in detail and how to work with them in therapy, the next chapter outlines some basic principles that are relevant to all therapies, whether or not those therapies take an emotion focus.

3
Therapy

In this chapter, we make some preliminary remarks about common factors that operate across all types of therapies, irrespective of whether the different therapies acknowledge such factors, before going on to consider the specifics of *Emotion-Focused Cognitive Therapy* in the next chapter.

Most people have one or two friends in their social networks who are good to talk to and who provide sound advice (unless of course you are a professional therapist in which case most of your social network may consist of other therapists – unfortunately!). These individuals have some of the skilful qualities that one would expect good therapists to possess (Frank, 1982), so this chapter provides an overview of these common factors in therapy and in therapists. We do this by arguing that therapy can be best considered in terms of three phases (Power, 2002; Power & Freeman, 2007). The three phases are summarized as follows.

The first phase is the development of a trusting relationship between the therapist and the client. For example, you meet a stranger on a train and within no time at all, you seem to be talking about the most personal issues troubling you, as if you had known this stranger for most of your life. So what are the qualities and factors relevant to building a good therapeutic alliance from the start of therapy? And how does the therapist handle conflicts in the alliance that result from holidays, or not meeting the demands of the client, or unsuccessful challenges, or other setbacks in therapy? Of course, many other sub-sidiary tasks occur at the beginning of therapy – the therapist must make some assessment of the client's presenting problem, understand key points in the client's history and begin to develop a formulation in which there is a judgement about the possibility of an intervention for the problem focus. However, unless all these tasks occur in the context of a trusting relationship between the client and the therapist, all the other tasks are likely to be undermined

The second phase of therapy is what we have labelled the 'work phase', in which the real business of short-term therapies gets done (and it is the phase that goes on forever in the very long-term thera-pies!). The actual work depends on a mix of the problem focus and the type of therapy, so that this phase most distinguishes the dif-ferent therapies from each other. For example, in cognitive therapy for depression, the client completes activity schedules and struc-tured diaries as homework exercises that are then brought back into therapy sessions and are worked on to identify negative automatic thoughts (NATs) and logical errors of thinking that can eventu-ally be reinterpreted in more functional ways. As we will see, in emotion-focused cognitive therapy the focus shifts away from the cognitions – the NATS and CATs – towards the actual problematic emotions, how these are experienced or avoided, what effects they have on significant others (including the therapist) and how these emotions can be more appropriately expressed or regulated. This emotion focus does not ignore the cognitive factors, but these are considered in terms of the SPAARS model as the relevant appraisals that generate the emotions, the interpersonal contexts in which they occur and beliefs and assumptions about emotions and emotion regulation both for self and significant others. The linking theme through all of the work is the focus on the problematic moods and emotions.

The third phase is the 'termination phase'. It is the most poorly dealt-with phase in the cognitive behavioural therapies (CBTs) and in many of the other short-term psychotherapies, with the recent excep-tion of interpersonal psychotherapy (Klerman et al., 1984; Weissman et al., 2000). This avoidance of termination issues in CBT is partic-ularly surprising because issues about termination are present from the start in a short-term therapy, in which there may be no opportu-nity to assess the client's reactions to therapy breaks such as holidays. Given also that the focus of therapy for many depressed clients may well be the unpredictability or loss of significant relationships, it is doubly surprising that CBT has been so poor at dealing with this phase. Only recently have CBT therapists come to consider relapse prevention strategies (Segal et al., 2001), but even here the focus is on how the client will deal with future difficulties rather than with their feelings about their relationship with the therapist coming to an end. One begins to suspect that the stereotypical CBT therapist is emotion avoidant and that the focus on cognition is used to deny the painful affect which may be directed at the therapist.

Before we consider these three phases in detail, a few words need to be said first about the issues of common factors in therapy and some of the ideas about the possibility of therapy integration (see Holmes & Bateman, 2002, for a fuller discussion of these issues).

Common Factors in Therapy

Part of the impetus for the exploration of integrative approaches to psychotherapy has arisen from the failure of many studies of the effectiveness of different therapies to find significant differences in outcome. Stiles et al. (1986) have labelled this the paradox of 'outcome equivalence contrasted with content non-equivalence'. It is clear from content analyses of therapy sessions that therapists of different persuasions do different things that are broadly consistent with the type of therapy to which they adhere (DeRubeis, et al. 1982; Luborsky et al., 1985). Nevertheless, despite the difference in content, the results from a broad range of studies are consistent with the proposal that no one therapy is ascendant over any other; thus, in the meta-analytic studies in which the results from large numbers of different studies are combined statistically, the general conclusion has been that all therapies are more effective than no treatment whatsoever, but there is little to distinguish amongst the therapies themselves. To give one example of a meta-analytic study, Robinson et al. (1990) combined the results from 58 studies of psychotherapy for depression in which at least one type of psychotherapy had been assessed against a waiting-list control group or a 'placebo' control group. The results showed that psychotherapies were substantially better than control groups both at immediate post treatment assessment and at follow-up. Furthermore, the initial apparent superiority of cognitive behavioural interventions over dynamic and interpersonal ones disappeared once the allegiance of the therapists taking part in the treatment was taken account of statistically.

Stiles et al. (1986) further argued that outcome equivalence applies not only to areas such as depression but also to areas where 'clinical wisdom' might suggest otherwise; for example, such wisdom would suggest that behavioural and cognitive behavioural methods are more effective than other forms of therapies for the treatment of phobias. The evidence for this proposal arises from analogue studies with subclinical populations (primarily students), but, they argued, it is less clear-cut in clinical trials.

To illustrate the problems that have arisen from the general failure to find differential effectiveness of therapy outcome, the National Institute of Mental Health (NIMH) Collaborative Depression study, which was the largest of its kind, will be considered as a specific example (Elkin et al., 1989). Of the 28 therapists working at three sites, 8 were cognitive behavioural, 10 were interpersonal therapists and a further 10 psychiatrists managed two pharmacotherapy conditions, one being imipramine plus 'clinical management', the other being placebo plus 'clinical management'. Of those patients meeting the criteria for major depressive disorder, 250 were randomly allocated between the four conditions. The therapies were manualized and considerable training and supervision occurred both before and throughout the trial by leading authorities for each therapy (see Shaw & Wilson-Smith, 1988). Elkin et al. (1989) reported that all four groups improved approximately equally well on the main symptom outcome measures. Perhaps the most surprising result was the extent of the improvement in the placebo plus clinical management group, which substantially outperformed control groups in most other studies, though a post hoc analysis showed that it was less effective for patients with more severe depressive disorders. Imber et al. (1990) have further shown that by and large treatments had no specific effects on measures such as the Dysfunctional Attitude Scale on which, for example, the cognitive therapy condition would have been expected to have more impact than the other treatments.

In summary, there are a rapidly increasing number of therapies, which, by analogy with languages, share many common factors or basic underlying principles. This proposal does not deny that therapists of different persuasions can be distinguished by what they say and do in therapy. A puzzle that has arisen from the vast array of psychotherapy outcome research is the general lack of differential effectiveness of treatments despite their technical diversity. As discussed earlier, one of the most dramatic examples of this effect is the NIMH study in which the least 'active' of all the treatments, the placebo plus clinical management condition, performed almost as well as the other conditions. Results such as these point to the operation of powerful common factors and individual therapist effects that swamp whatever treatment effects might exist. In the remainder of this chapter we consider how such factors might be viewed, beginning first with a look at the prospects for *theoretical* integration from a CBT or emotion-focused perspective.

Therapy Integration

At first sight, the proposal that there could be an integrative therapeutic framework might seem ludicrous given both the diversity of therapeutic practice and the hostility that exists between different approaches. How, for example, could behavioural exposure be in any way similar to transference resolution? The argument to be pursued here is that this is not the appropriate level at which to state the problem. Instead, by analogy with the discussion of 'low level' and 'high level' semantics earlier, a focus on specific techniques or on specific types of intervention may lead one to ignore a higher level of meaning in which these diverse techniques and types of intervention share common aims and purposes. What will be proposed is that first there is a common context in which therapies occur, that is, the therapeutic relationship. Second, that there is a common mechanism of change, the transformation of meaning, through which all interventions proceed. Of course, there are numerous other stage theories of therapy (e.g. Beitman, 1992; Prochaska & Diclemente, 1992; Stiles et al., 1990); the present summary is consistent with the broad view of these previous theories, while differing in the details.

The framework outlined in Table 3.1 shows, as noted earlier, that any type of therapy can be viewed in terms of three phases (see Power, 2002). In the first phase, the primary task is the building of an alliance with the client or patient; thus, despite other subsidiary tasks such as assessment and formulation, it may be pointless entering into the work of therapy unless a therapeutic alliance develops because the

Table 3.1   Three phases of therapy

	Phase 1	*Phase 2*	*Phase 3*
Primary task	Alliance	Work	Termination
Secondary tasks	Problem assessment	Tasks performance	Relapse prevention
	General assessment Formulation	Interpretation Challenge	Self-therapy Use of social network
	Sharing therapy rationale	Transference development Problem reformulation	Transference resolution

work is likely to fail. The second phase, or the work phase, is where differences between therapies are most dramatic. The third phase is the termination of therapy. Again, therapies and therapists differ considerably on how termination is dealt with, but we would argue that the issues and problems remain the same irrespective of therapy type. Before the details of these phases are spelt out however, there is a short digression to consider more traditional approaches to common factors in psychotherapies. The traditional approach is best summarized in the series of handbooks that have been edited over the years by Garfield and Bergin (Garfield & Bergin, 1978, 1986; Lambert, 2004) and which have exhaustively detailed research into therapist, client and therapy factors. Work on therapist factors was best exemplified by research into client-centred therapy (Rogers, 1957) and the proposed holy trinity of warmth, empathy and genuineness (Truax & Carkhuff, 1967), which every therapist was supposed to possess. However, the early optimism that characterized this work eventually gave way to the realization that even 'ideal' therapists had patients they did not get on well with and that the mere presence of such factors was not sufficient for therapeutic change. As Stiles et al. (1986) concluded, 'the earlier hope of finding a common core in the therapist's personal qualities or behaviour appears to have faded' (p.175).

Work on client variables has in the past been characterized by the examination of lists of sociodemographic and personality variables (see Garfield, 1978), from which it has been possible to conclude very little. In a re-examination of the issue, Beutler (1991) concluded that there still has been little development in our understanding of client variables. Following a summary of some of the major variables that might be examined, Beutler also pointed out:

> There are nearly one and one-half million potential combinations of therapy, therapist, phase, and patient types that must be studied in order to rule out relevant differences among treatment types (p. 229).

Fewer than 100 methodologically sound studies have been carried out to test these possible interactions! Some promising leads from investigations of client attitudes and expectations, however, provide a more sophisticated view of such variables. For example, Caine et al. (1981) found that the type of model that clients had of their problems (e.g. medical vs. psychological) and the direction of their main interests ('inner-directed' vs. 'outer-directed') predicted dropout rates and outcome in psychotherapy.

Work on specific therapy factors has also run aground on the problems of finding any differential effects (Stiles et al., 1986). Some of these problems were raised earlier in the 'Introduction' in which the pattern of outcome equivalence of psychotherapies for a range of disorders was outlined. There may possibly be advances in this area in the future with the use of so-called dismantling, in which one or more of the putative 'active' ingredients of a therapy are dropped in some of the conditions and the manualization of therapies, combined with measures of treatment adherence, ensure that something like the therapy in question is actually taking place. However, as the NIMH Collaborative Depression study illustrated (see 'Common Factors in Therapy'), the fact that some therapists did extremely well and some not so well, irrespective of the type of therapy demonstrates that therapy factors will only emerge in interaction with other therapist and client variables rather than as main effects. A specific example of this point comes from the Sheffield psychotherapy project carried out by David Shapiro and his colleagues. The initial published analyses of this project showed an advantage for prescriptive (i.e. cognitive behavioural) therapy over exploratory (i.e. psychodynamic) therapy in the treatment of stressed managers. However, a later reanalysis (Shapiro et al., 1989) found that this advantage was true for one of the principal therapists involved in the study, but the second therapist was equally effective with both types of therapy. In an interesting conclusion, Shapiro et al. (1989) turned on its head the initial question of which brand of therapy was better, as follows:

> The present findings are broadly consistent with the clinical lore that each new therapist should try different approaches to find the one in which he or she is most effective (p. 385).

Rather than examining these separate lists of therapist, therapy and client factors any further, we now return to the suggested framework (see Table 3.1) in which all therapies can be considered and examine the factors in interaction with each other.

Alliance and Misalliance

The importance of the alliance between therapist and patient arose early in the psychoanalytic literature. Freud (1912) viewed the alliance as the healthy part of the transference, a proposal that was later extended by other psychoanalytic writers. Carl Rogers (1957) also focused on the importance of the therapeutic relationship, though the client-centred view is different from the psychoanalytic. The diverse influences on the origins of the concept and the growing awareness of its importance in CBT (e.g. Safran & Segal, 1990) make it a cosmopolitan concept which has the advantage that therapists of different orientations can begin to talk to each other because of a shared language. Fortunately, this problem is not insurmountable; as Wolfe and Goldfried (1988) stated:

> The therapeutic alliance is probably the quintessential integrative variable because its importance does not lie within the specifications of one school of thought (p. 449).

To understand the concept, the three factors proposed by Bordin (1979) provide a reasonable starting point – that there should be a bond between the therapist and the patient, that there should be an agreement on goals and that there should be an agreement on tasks. In addition, the work of Jerome Frank (1982) provides a more general framework from which to view both the therapeutic relationship and the whole question of common factors in psychotherapy. To quote:

> The efficacy of all procedures . . .depends on the establishment of a good therapeutic relationship between the patient and the therapist. No method works in the absence of this relationship (p. 15).

Frank goes on to describe many shared components that help to strengthen the relationship with the patient and which help the patient to have more positive expectations. To highlight a couple of these components:

A confiding relationship

The patient should be able to trust and talk to the therapist about painful issues without feeling judged. These issues may be ones that the patient is 'confessing' for the first time. This feature of confiding is not of course unique to therapeutic relationships, but is a characteristic of any confiding relationship (Power et al., 1988). A problem that has been identified in poor therapeutic relationships is that the confiding and expression of negative feelings by the patient is responded to with hostility by the therapist; the outcome of such therapy is often unsuccessful (Henry et al., 1986).

> Ms. H was a 28-year-old single woman who within minutes of the beginning of the first session began shouting and banging her fists on the arms of her chair and the wall next to her. This behaviour did in fact occur spasmodically over several sessions and declined only gradually. My initial reaction was both shock and fear and the thought that I needed to run for cover. Fortunately I didn't run but weathered the onslaught, though the embarrassed stares after sessions of my colleagues in adjoining offices was somewhat harder to cope with! Amongst other things, Ms. H was angry because she had been given a male therapist when she had wanted a female therapist. It turned out that she had previously had a female therapist who was so frightened of her that Ms. H. had no respect for her and so made no progress whatsoever. The alliance subsequently developed because I was able to take her hostility without either becoming hostile in return or becoming frozen with fear.

The development of an alliance with Ms. H was of course a key part of the effectiveness of the therapy, because the patient comes to experience a relationship that is not dominated by one or other partner and in which impulses and emotion often experienced as overwhelming or damaging by the patient is contained in a safe manner by the therapist. The patient thereby can learn to experience such affect as safe and containable.

A rationale

Patients should be provided with a framework within which to understand their distress together with an outline of the principles behind the therapy and what treatment might involve from a practical point of view. Failure to provide such a rationale may leave the client mystified or anxious with misconceptions about what might or might not happen. As a consequence, there is a risk that the client could drop out of therapy prematurely. The CBTs are particularly strong on providing such rationales; for example, the *Coping with Depression* and *Coping with Anxiety* booklets are typically handed to patients after one or two sessions of cognitive therapy as a homework assignment. Indeed, Fennell and Teasdale (1987) reported that a positive response to the *Coping with Depression* booklet was a good indicator of positive outcome in cognitive therapy.

One of the points that must also be dealt with in therapy is the likelihood, as in real life, of the development of 'misalliances'. Some of these misalliances may be temporary and resolvable if dealt with, whereas others may require referral on to another agency or other drastic action. As a starting point from which to consider misalliances, we can consider again Bordin's (1979) three components of the therapeutic alliance – the bond, the goals and the tasks – of which all or any can be implicated in a misalliance. It is well recognized that some patients are more difficult to develop an alliance with than others; thus, the extension of cognitive therapy into work with personality disorder individuals has helped to heighten awareness of the therapeutic relationship amongst cognitive therapists together with a re-examination of several related psychodynamic issues (Beck et al, 2004; Linehan, 1993). Less intractable misalliances occur when for example the patient attends therapy to appease someone else such as a spouse or partner or professional such as a GP, or the patient expects physical treatment rather than psychotherapy, or is attending because of a court order. Through careful discussion of the relevant issues the therapist should be able to identify these types of misalliances.

Even when a satisfactory alliance has been established, the painful work of therapy can lead to 'ruptures' (Gaston et al., 1995); for example, a behavioural exposure session that goes wrong and becomes too anxiety provoking can lead to a setback in the relationship that needs to be addressed before continuing with the therapeutic work. Other factors such as breaks in therapy for holidays, an approaching therapy termination and so on can also lead to problems in the alliance that need to be dealt with explicitly and sensitively.

Of course, any psychoanalytic therapist reading this account is likely to respond 'So what – we've known this all along'. The point is that until recently CBT therapists have simply concentrated on Phase 2, the work phase (see Table 3.1) and ignored Phase 1, the alliance. Clinical reality and the extension of the CBT approach to work with more intractable problems have led to a re-evaluation of this piece of short-sightedness.

The Work Phase

The second phase of therapy identified in Table 3.1 is the work phase. The differences between schools of therapy are clearest in this phase, yet it is possible that even here there may be common factors that link this diversity. Perhaps the most dramatic difference is that claimed by Carl Rogers for his client-centred psychotherapy (Rogers, 1957) for which he claimed that there was no work phase because the mechanism of change was through the unconditional positive regard from the therapist (i.e. all Phase 1). However, this claim ignores the fact that work occurs even when the therapist is non-directive. As stated earlier, there is no doubt that the textbook differences between different types of therapy are reflected in practice in therapy itself, and, furthermore, that the same therapist acts differently with different patients, or even with the same patient at different points in therapy (Luborsky et al., 1982). To consider an example, the typical sequence in cognitive therapy for depression might consist of something similar to that shown in Figure 3.1. Behavioural tasks are set initially both to increase the activity level and the day-to-day experience of success of the depressed individual. The second stage consists of the identification of NATs and the construction of rational responses to obviate their mood-worsening consequences, whereas the third stage consists of the identification of underlying dysfunctional assumptions, which are challenged through a variety of techniques such as *in vivo* experiments that test out faulty assumptions. Although this apparent neat sequence may be very useful for teaching purposes and may even be useful once in a while clinically, it is inconceivable, as argued earlier, that a coherent psychological model could work with

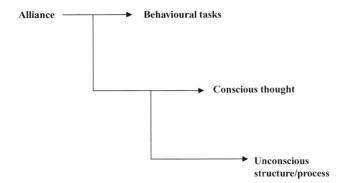

Figure 3.1   A typical sequence for cognitive therapy for depression

independent processing systems of this variety (Power & Dalgleish, 2008). It seems likely that the mechanism of change may be the same for all three 'steps' in this sequence; thus, for the individual to perform behavioural tasks successfully, change may be necessary at both a conscious and an unconscious level: Remember that the individual is simply carrying out tasks that used to be carried out; therefore, the crucial factor is the loss of inhibition of positive thought and action, the 'loss of the positive' that is typical in depression. The gist of this argument is the viewpoint that behavioural change cannot occur without underlying cognitive change and, especially if the person is unable to report the behavioural change, it implies that the change has occurred at an underlying automatic or unconscious cognitive level.

Perhaps a more dramatic attempt to analyse the similarities rather than the differences in the work phase is portrayed in Table 3.2. This table takes each of the cornerstone techniques from behaviour therapy, psychoanalysis and cognitive therapy, namely, behavioural exposure, transference resolution and the challenging of dysfunctional assumptions and asks similar questions of each. To take the first point shown in the table, the three approaches differ in the extent to which they focus on childhood, but it is commonplace to identify the original source of the problem in childhood, whether it is the learning of phobic reactions from primary caretakers, the repression of forbidden wishes and impulses or the development of self-critical attitudes. The procedures by which these issues are explored are astonishing because of their similarity given the traditional hostility and rivalry between the approaches; in each case, the patient is encouraged to a heightened emotional response in the presence of the

Table 3.2 A summary of psychotherapy techniques

Therapeutic technique	*Problem origin*	*Procedure*	*Putative mechanism of change*
Exposure	Learning, typically in childhood (traumatic, observational, information transmission)	Heighten emotion with relevant object/situation in therapist's presence	Extinction Relearning Coping
Transference	Childhood experience in relation to significant others	Heighten emotional reaction to therapist as object	Working through to realistic perception of therapist
Challenging dysfunctional assumptions	Childhood experience in relation to significant others	Heighten emotion to person, situation or object	Reinterpret Reconstruct

particular object, person or situation (see later chapters also). In psychoanalysis, the therapist encourages this reaction towards himself or herself, but in principle the mechanism seems similar. Cognitive therapists might argue that it is the cognitive *belief* rather than the emotional reaction that is being accessed, but, as we discussed in Chapter 2, more recent views of the relationship between cognition and emotion reject such a simplistic linear causal view in that cognition and emotion are viewed as mutually interdependent (Power & Dalgleish, 2008). More correctly therefore, the argument is that therapy heightens access to cognitive–emotional structures and processes that relate to past and present significant objects and significant others including the therapist. In the context of this heightened access, there is the common therapeutic goal that patients will relearn, cope more successfully with, view more realistically, reinterpret or reconstruct; that is, in some way view more constructively the object, person or situation that has been the source of their distress or conflict.

An interesting addendum to this discussion comes from a study reported by Goldsamt et al. (1992) which consisted of a content analysis of a video produced to illustrate the therapeutic approaches of Beck (i.e. Beckian cognitive therapy), Meichenbaum (i.e. Meichenbaum's form of CBT), and Strupp (psychodynamic therapy). In this video, these three well-known therapists each interview the same patient, named 'Richard', to illustrate their therapeutic approaches. The results of the content analyses showed unexpectedly that Meichenbaum and Strupp were more similar to each other than they were to Beck, rather than finding the predicted similarity between Beck and Meichenbaum; thus, results showed that Meichenbaum and Strupp both tended to focus on the patient's impact on other people, but Beck focused more on the impact other people had on the patient. The moral is, in re-emphasis of what has long been well known in the therapy literature – the purported differences in therapy should not be based on what therapists say they do, but, rather, on what they actually do; the contrast can be considerable (Sloane et al., 1975).

The Termination Phase

The termination phase can often be the most avoided and most difficult phase of therapy, especially for the trainee therapist. It may, for example, be the phase when the therapist's fantasies of omnipotent healing face the reality of only minor therapeutic gain; when guilt about premature termination is avoided by therapist and patient alike to the detriment of therapy or when the sadness and anger at the loss of a close relationship are avoided because they are too painful. For whatever reason therefore, this phase requires a healthy honesty which is not dealt with adequately in the CBT literature because of the traditional focus on technical skill rather than the therapeutic relationship.

Paradoxically, the termination phase in short-term therapies may be more difficult to manage than in longer-term therapies. One reason for this difficulty, as noted earlier, is that longer-term therapies may have had numerous breaks that provide important information about how the patient will cope with termination, for example, whether the patient avoids discussing an upcoming break and the extent to which the alliance is disrupted following a break. In short-term therapies, there may never have been any breaks, and the therapist may mistakenly believe that there is insufficient time to deal with termination issues. In fact, given that cognitive therapy was designed as a short-term therapy for depression (Beck et al., 1979), the central depressive concerns about dependency and loss imply that an approaching termination will reawaken these areas of conflict and should therefore be actively and explicitly dealt with by the therapist.

There are of course a range of assessment measures which the cognitive behaviour therapist in particular will perhaps use if information is needed to help decide whether the patient is ready to finish therapy. Most of these measures are well known and include a range of self-report indices of symptom levels, dysfunctional attitudes, automatic thoughts, activity levels and achievement of therapeutic aims. However, in view of the traditional behavioural ambivalence about self-report noted earlier, it is surprising that CBT therapists rely so heavily on measures reactive to factors such as the range of self-report biases, the need to please the therapist, etc. It is surprising that there has not been greater development of behavioural performance measures and psychophysiological indices such as heart rate and galvanic skin response (Power, 1991). However, in addition to the self-report, behavioural and psychophysiological measures, there are also several other ways in which therapists can gauge the readiness of patients for the termination of therapy. One of these is when the patient has internalized a positive model of the therapist (Casement, 1985). Evidence for such models comes, for example, from reports of imaginary dialogues that the patient holds with the therapist between sessions: 'I was just about to leap over the checkout in the supermarket in absolute panic, when I stopped and wondered what you would say to me in such a situation. . .' Such imaginary dialogues are a sign that the therapeutic work is actively continuing outside of sessions; they also provide the therapist with clues about the type of therapist model that the patient has internalized (Power, 2007). This process of internalization can be encouraged in sessions when in response to questions from the patient such as 'What do you think I should do about such-and-such?' the therapist can encourage the patient to construct a reply 'Well, what do you think my answer might be to this question?'.

A second interpersonal measure is to assess the patient's way of relating to significant others in his or her social network. It is well known that the majority of neurotic and psychotic problems remain untreated in the community, as shown for example in the various papers from the large Epidemiologic Catchment Area study (Bourdon et al., 1988; Myers et al., 1984). A reasonable hypothesis is that a key difference between referred and non-referred cases lies in the quality of support available in the individual's network (Frank, 1982), a factor that might also explain the originally unexpected finding that the outcome of schizophrenia was better in the developing rather than the developed countries (World Health Organization, 1979). One of the largely unexplored areas of therapy outcome may be therefore whether, following progress in therapy, patients make better use of their social networks, whether they relate in healthier ways to key individuals in their networks and whether they have the capacity to establish new healthy relationships particularly if significant role-relationships are missing. This type of assessment can either be made using established measures of the quality of social support (Power et al., 1988) or can be undertaken informally with the patient. A key question therefore is whether the patient, with or without a 'therapeutic' significant other, has the capacity and motivation to establish new healthier relationships that will replace the relationship with the therapist. The following is an example of a change in a relationship with a significant other and the subsequent effects on how the patient related to others in her network:

> Ms. H, who was also referred to earlier, was in a permanent state of anger with everybody, or so it seemed. This anger was expressed against everyone apart from her mother with whom, she stated categorically, she had never been angry. It transpired that her mother had a self-diagnosed heart condition and a range of other symptoms with which she had manipulated and blackmailed her family for many years. Ms. H firmly believed that if she got angry with her mother, her mother would die. Ms. H's belief in this murderous anger was first put to the test in the therapeutic relationship in which I had managed to contain her anger and survive. After about six months of therapy, and with great trepidation, she eventually got angry with her mother for the first time. As the considerable backlog of anger eventually came out, so she felt less angry with other people. One of the first people she became close to was her younger sister who, she found, had similar views and difficulties herself. It also turned out that her mother's 'heart condition' had not been diagnosed by any specialist, though her mother had failed to mention this fact to her family.

One final health warning should be issued for therapists who find themselves unable to finish therapy with their clients. Stieper and Weiner (1959) reported a study of so-called interminable pa-tients who had been seen in therapy for a long time in a particular clinic. They found that these patients tended to be restricted to a few therapists, that the therapists involved tended to have unrealistic aims for what the patients might achieve and that they also had excessive needs to be appreciated both in their role as therapists and in their private lives. In a dramatic intervention in this study, the administrators of the clinic discharged the patients concerned against the wishes of the therapists! Follow-up showed that they subsequently did no worse than any of the other patients. Not a study to mention to your local psychology services manager by the way.

Final Comments and Conclusions

The conclusion that there are no significant differences between the various types of therapy is one that attempts to prove the null hypothesis, which, as any statistically minded individual will tell you, is not the way to proceed in research. In fact, the appearance of such a conclusion as a consequence of meta-analytic studies or large-outcome studies such as the NIMH Collaborative Depression study necessitates many important qualifications of this 'all have won' and therefore 'anybody-can-do-anything' conclusion. One of the most crucial qualifications relates to the therapist's skill in establishing a therapeutic alliance. Evidence suggests that therapists of all persuasions have particular difficulty with patients who are negative and express hostility in therapy; the failure to establish an alliance may be the most important factor that contributes to negative outcome in therapy, that is, the fact that some patients get worse rather than better. However, it may only be when a therapeutic alliance is established that additional effects of specific techniques for specific problems can emerge. Even outcome studies that manualize treatments and assess therapist adherence to these treatments do not generally assess factors such as the quality of the alliance or other factors common to all therapies.

At a more general level, the hope that there might one day be a grand unified theory is, as in physics, a long way off. Nevertheless, there are positive signs: A broad-based cognitive model seems capable of incorporating the strengths of both traditional learning approaches and psychoanalysis while overcoming some of their limitations (Power & Dalgleish, 2008). Any such cognitive model is substantially different from the current models that underpin CBT approaches as we argued previously because of the need to incorporate both modern learning theory and a cognitive version of the dynamic unconscious. The theory also needs to provide a framework in which to view the great diversity and ever-increasing number of psychotherapies. Only then will we understand what distinguishes the *good* underwater massage therapist from the *bad* behaviour therapist – and vice versa – and understand why each may be useful in the right place.

Finally, it should be noted that in terms of the history of the psychotherapy integration movement, the approach taken here is an example of the common factors and theoretical integration viewpoint (Norcross & Goldfried, 1992). Although many therapists now adopt a so-called technical eclecticism, in that they may use techniques and procedures from different approaches without adopting a particular theory, our approach has been to argue strongly for the possibility of theoretical integration (Power & Dalgleish, 1997, 2008). As noted throughout this chapter, the CBT approach already represents an integration of behavioural and cognitive viewpoints, which have at times in the past been at war with each other. Part of this integration has occurred because practitioners ignored some of the earlier theoretical arguments. Hopefully, the more recent integrative theories will equal clinical experience in their richness and offer further hope of progress. To this integration however we offer the third missing ingredient: emotion. We believe that CBT will make its next major advance if it has an emotion focus. The remainder of this book therefore tries to demonstrate how clinical practice can develop with the addition of emotion.

4
The Assessment of Emotion

The clinical world is full of scales and measures that purport to measure emotions and moods. On a regular basis we hand our clients measures of depression, anxiety, obsessive-compulsive disorder, post-traumatic stress disorder (PTSD) or whatever, and assume that they do a reasonable job of measuring the problematic state because that is the measure we have always used and that is the tradition of measurement for that clinical group. Perhaps as clinicians we are less concerned that the measure contains 'stray' items that do not relate to the concept or that the items have to be changed with each new edition of the *Diagnostic and Statistical Manual (DSM)* according to the whims of the committee that reviewed that particular diagnostic category – a category that, of course, has no theoretical basis because the *DSM* is based on consensus rather than theory. Perhaps as clinicians we are prepared to live in such an inconsistent world so long as we are seen to be keeping up with the latest clinical fashions.

But why should we be? Surely, even as clinicians when we use something, we want to know that it is reliable and valid. You do not have to know the inner workings of the car engine to know that you want a reliable car that will get you from A to B – why would we want a car where one of the wheels might fall off, where the brake lights were under the bonnet rather than at the rear of the car or where you ended up in C rather than B? Well, many of the measures and the assessments that clinicians currently use have exactly these problems, as we spend some time demonstrating in this chapter. We also propose a shift to a theoretically driven assessment system based on emotion and emotion regulation, whilst using the best of the rest until something better comes along. To continue with the car analogy, there is no point in improving the petrol engine if the world is about to run out of petrol.

Examples of the Mess

Let us consider some examples of the mess that we have gotten ourselves into. We start with a brief review of the *DSM* category of depressive disorder and the equivalent *International Classification of Diseases and Related Health Problems (ICD)* category of Depressive Episode (see Table 4.1).

In his account of the mess called 'depression', Bebbington (2004) points out that whilst *DSM* requires one of the 'key' symptoms listed in Table 4.1 with a total of five symptoms, *ICD* requires two of its 'key'

Table 4.1   *DSM* and *ICD* criteria for depression

DSM-IV	*ICD-10*
Key symptoms	Key symptoms
Depressed mood	Depressed mood
Anhedonia	Anhedonia
	Fatigue/loss of energy
Additional symptoms	Additional Symptoms:
Fatigue/loss of energy	Weight/appetite change
Weight/appetite loss/gain	Sleep disturbance
Insomnia/hypersomnia	Agitation/retardation
Agitation/retardation	Low esteem/confidence
Low self-esteem/guilt	Self reproach/guilt
Impaired thinking/concentration	Impaired thinking/concentration
Suicidal thoughts	Suicidal thoughts
Criteria	Criteria
One key, five symptoms total	Two key, four symptoms total
Distress/social impairment	

Source: Bebbington (2004, p. 6).

symptoms with a total of four symptoms for 'mild episodes' or eight symptoms for 'severe episodes'. So here are two example symptom profiles for the diagnosis of depression:

Depression 1 (DSM): *depressed mood, appetite loss, insomnia, guilt, suicidal thought*

Depression 2 (ICD): *anhedonia, fatigue, retardation, impaired concentration.*

Although both these individuals are classified as 'depressed', they do not have a single common symptom. In fact, we have just completed Beck Depression Inventory II (BDI-II) (Beck et al., 1996), the main self-report measure of depression, for both these cases; the *DSM* depression person came out with a total score of 36 and the *ICD* one with a score of 28. Both these BDI scores indicate a degree of severity of the depressions, but they have completely different profiles of scores across the two respondents, even though the BDI is a *DSM*-based measure and has been revised to mirror the changes for depression in *DSM-IV*.

If you thought this situation could not get any worse, please tighten your seat belts! Not only do the two main diagnostic systems produce the equivalent labels for people who do not have a single symptom in common, but when it comes to emotion *both* of the diagnostic systems get it completely wrong! That is, although both *DSM* and *ICD* focus on the role of *guilt* in relation to depression, recent analyses of depression have suggested that *shame* may be more important and that the role of guilt has been overplayed (Andrews, 1995; Power & Dalgleish, 1997; Tangney, 1999). Because the BDI is a *DSM*-based measure, it also gets the analysis wrong – there is no 'shame' item on the most widely used assessment measure of depression, only a 'guilt' item. It is also worth noting that few, if any, of the depression measures adequately assess the interpersonal component of depression.

To explore the potential roles of guilt and shame, we carried out a study of a group of individuals presenting to a psychology clinic with depression, anxiety or both (Power & Tarsia, 2007). Amongst a number of procedures, they were asked to complete the Basic Emotions Scale (BES) (Power, 2006) which is presented in detail later in the chapter. In statistical analyses, we found that the recent self-reported levels of both guilt and shame (or self-disgust) were correlated with the severity of depression when included separately in the analyses, but only the level of shame remained predictive when both were included in a multiple regression analysis together. That is, shame rather than guilt is more important both statistically and conceptually in relation to depression. Shame of course is a much more all-encompassing and aversive emotion than guilt, but the fact that *DSM* and *ICD* have missed its importance in depression and in other types of psychopathology adds to their already sorry list of failures.

The problem identified here is not limited to the case of depression. For many years, Richard Bentall (2003) and others have argued that the diagnostic category of 'schizophrenia' has similar problems of reliability and validity and that the diagnosis can refer to two people with completely different symptom profiles. He has cogently argued that the best way forward is to consider the next level, where people share important clusters of symptoms, such as those clustered around auditory hallucinations or delusional belief systems, given that the interventions required for such clusters, whether pharmacological or psychological, might be very different depending on whether the primary problems are centred on hallucinations or on delusions. As an aside, we note that the role of emotion both in the aetiology and course of schizophrenia-type disorders has been considerably underestimated, though it is beyond the scope of the current book to set this record straight.

Again, we must emphasize that the problem with the diagnostic systems is not limited to depression or even to schizophrenia, as the following examples illustrate.

Frank was referred by his GP because he had anxiety problems. On the Spielberger State-Trait Anxiety Inventory (STAI) he scored 32 on trait, which placed him well within the low-anxiety range. However, Frank had begun to experience panic attacks at work, which he found extremely distressing, because, as he stated, he had always been a calm and collected person and could never understand when other people got anxious.

Victor was referred with PTSD by his GP. PTSD is classified in *DSM* as an anxiety disorder, but Victor scored 6 on the Beck Anxiety Inventory (BAI), which placed him within the normal range. He had been a soldier in Iraq and come to disagree with the US–UK policy.

He felt angry with George Bush and Tony Blair for taking them into Iraq; in fact, he felt angry with everybody he came across. Anxiety was not his problem, but anger certainly was.

Irina scored 38 on the BDI-II (i.e. higher than either of the two 'depressed' cases considered earlier), but said that she was not particularly depressed because she had known what depression was like when she was younger. She scored 16 on the BAI and had been referred with Obsessive-compulsive disorder, which is also classified by *DSM* as an 'anxiety disorder'. Irina spent most of her time washing herself and disinfecting her flat because of her fear of AIDS contamination and was unable to allow any visitors in case she became contaminated.

Mary also had an elevated score on the BDI-II of 29 and stated that she was not depressed. Mary currently suffered from bulimia and had other disorders in the past, including anorexia and episodes of self-harm. Unfortunately, the role of emotion in the eating disorders is also vastly underestimated, a problem that we return to in later chapters.

These examples are provided only to illustrate the range of problems that exist with current diagnostic and classification systems, and therefore the problems that result from assessment measures that are typically based on the classification systems and are in widespread use.

As a final example, and to illustrate that it is not just psychiatry and the classification systems that get it wrong, we consider the Positive and Negative Affect Scale (PANAS) (Watson et al., 1988), which is a widely used scale for current mood assessment in psychology. Table 4.2 shows the 20 items that constitute the PANAS together with our best guess about which emotion the item attempts to assess. Despite being very generous, only 15 of the 20 items are related to emotion, and, as summarized in Table 4.3, the coverage of some of the basic emotions is minimal and inadequate. Still, on the positive side, at the least the PANAS includes a shame item, which gives it one advantage over the BDI.

Before we consider some of the quantitative and qualitative assessments that clinicians and clinical researchers might use, we first consider emotions in relation to meta-emotional skills. We are all meant to experience emotions in their various forms and that is part of their universality; hence, it is what we do or do not do with these

Table 4.2   Items from the PANAS scale

PANAS item	Basic emotion
Interested	Happy (?)
Distressed	Sad
Excited	Happy
Upset	Sad; anger
Strong	?
Guilty	Disgust
Scared	Anxiety
Hostile	Anger
Enthusiastic	Happy (?)
Proud	Happy
Irritable	Anger
Alert	?
Ashamed	Disgust
Inspired	Happy (?)
Nervous	Anxiety
Determined	?
Attentive	?
Jittery	Anxiety
Active	?
Afraid	Anxiety

'?' indicates uncertainty.

emotions across the lifespan that makes them problematic. Therefore, to assess emotions fully, we must also assess the emotion regulation strategies that people use to moderate and influence their emotions (Gross, 2007).

Table 4.3   Emotion categorization of PANAS items

PANAS item	Basic emotion
Summary	
Happy	5
Sad	2
Anger	2
Disgust	2
Anxiety	4

Five items not inherently affective but represent cognitive or other states.

Emotions, Emotion Regulation and Meta-Emotional Skills

The publication of the book *Emotional Intelligence* by Daniel Goleman in 1995 led to the sudden popularization of the proposal for so-called emotional intelligence (EI) made by Salovey and Meyer (1990). This proposal was based on earlier ones such as Gardner's (1983) concept of social intelligence. The popularization has led to the assessment and teaching of emotional skills in the workplace and in schools, though academically, it remains mired in controversy. The main arguments against the proposal (Davies et al., 1998; Roberts et al., 2001) are that it offers nothing unique not already covered by the existing personality theory and approaches to intelligence. Our view is that the term 'emotional intelligence' is one that is best avoided because of its value-laden and elitist implications, but clearly there are variations in emotional skills that should not be ignored.

The development of emotional skills is evident throughout childhood (Izard, 2001), and there are developmental disorders such as autism that have been linked to deficits in *Theory of Mind* (Frith, 2003), and which therefore are, by definition, accompanied by deficits in emotional skills (Hobson, 1995). However, we prefer to refer to such skills as *meta-emotional skills* and associated *meta-emotional representations*, in parallel to the use of the term 'metacognition' in cognition and development first proposed by Flavell (1979). These meta-emotional skills are therefore likely to show a different pattern of population distribution than cognitive intelligence, which approximates the normal distribution curve, because of threshold effects consequent to problems and deficits that affect disorders such as autism and psychopathy. We acknowledge though that the term 'meta-emotional skill' may never have the same popular appeal and ring to it as that of EI and that Daniel Goleman is unlikely to write a book with this new title.

The key areas that are important in meta-emotional skills and representations include the perception and understanding of emotion in self and others, and the regulation of emotions again both in self and in others. The deficits seen in the autistic spectrum disorders lead to clear problems with the recognition of emotions in self and others, together with the additional complexity that such disorders occur in far greater numbers in males than in females (Baron-Cohen, 2004).

Such gender ratios do not imply though that all men are deficient in meta-emotional skills, contrary perhaps to some popular views, especially with the powerful cultural pressures on the gender-related expression of different emotions, and that can be seen in the reported experience of different emotions (Ekman, 1999; Scherer et al., 2001).

One of the most important areas of meta-emotional skills is that of emotion regulation. There have been many conceptualizations of emotion regulation (Carver & Scheier, 1990; Gross, 1998; Larsen, 2000; Philippot & Feldman, 2004). In a recent summary of his own approach, Gross (2007) has drawn together work showing how different regulation strategies can be applied at different points during the course of an emotional reaction. Even before an emotion begins, you can avoid a situation because you know it will be emotional, or you can try and stop the emotion once it starts through inhibiting yourself from expressing the emotion, or you could change the consequences of having expressed (or not expressed) an emotion. In Gross's influential approach, the emotion is broken down into a series of temporal stages with the possibility of different strategies being applied at each of the stages.

In contrast to Gross's approach, we take a more holistic approach to the regulation of emotion and believe that people tend to regulate all aspects of an emotion in a similar way; for example, if you have intense exam anxiety, you will avoid exams if at all possible, and if you do have to take an exam, you may do things to avoid the actual experience of the anxiety itself, such as by taking medication. The common feature here is the attempted *avoidance* of the situation and the emotional experience.

Our approach (Phillips & Power, 2007) has been to consider first that just as most emotions are primarily generated and experienced in an interpersonal context, many emotion regulation strategies are *inter*personal in addition to perhaps more familiar *intra*personal strategies. Examples of interpersonal strategies would include talking to a friend or getting advice, but other external strategies also exist that are not inherently interpersonal, such as doing something pleasant like shopping or sports. Examples of *internal* emotion regulation strategies include inhibiting the experience of the emotion and ruminating about the emotion so that it continues for longer than it otherwise would. We believe therefore that one important dimension along which emotion regulation should be considered is whether the strategies are *internal* or *external*. As an interesting aside, the internal–external dimension also maps on very well to the distinction between *internalizing* (e.g. depression) and *externalizing* (e.g. conduct disorders) disorders in children and adolescents (Casey, 1996), which has also been found to relate to early temperamental differences in children when followed up into their teenage years (Caspi et al., 1995).

A second dimension along which emotion regulation strategies can be grouped is, we propose, whether the strategies are *functional* or *dysfunctional*. Writers such as Gross (2007) argue against using categorizations that evaluate some strategies as more negative than others on the grounds that what may be seen as dysfunctional in one culture, subgroup, family or individual could be functional in another. However, we believe that there is a strong and well-supported tradition that goes back to both Sigmund Freud (1926) and his daughter Anna (Freud, 1937) in which the habitual use of certain defence mechanisms is seen to have problematic consequences for the individual both physically and psychologically. Some of these defence mechanisms, such as regression and dissociation, are more likely to be dysfunctional, whereas other defences, such as sublimation and suppression, are more likely to be functional. Moreover, there is now a wide range of research from diverse areas in support of this categorization. To cite but one example, George Vaillant's classic work (Vaillant, 1990) on the lifetime follow-up of a group of Harvard students dramatically demonstrated how health and even premature death were predicted by the typical defence mechanisms that they used as undergraduates. Perhaps as Pierre Philippot (2007) has emphasized, it is also about the *flexibility* with which emotion regulation strategies are used; for example, avoidance may be appropriate in some situations or contexts, but it becomes problematic if used excessively and inflexibly. Our meta-emotional skills therefore can help us to switch between regulation strategies as appropriate.

In summary, therefore, we have proposed that emotion regulation strategies can be usefully grouped along dimensions of internal–external and functional–dysfunctional. We acknowledge of course that under certain circumstances even the most apparently dysfunctional strategy can be functional; for example, dissociation during the experience of a traumatic event may permit the individual to function without being overwhelmed by anxiety and panic, similar to numbing during excess physical pain. However, the habitual use of dissociation is clearly dysfunctional, as Vaillant's (1990) work has

Table 4.4   A 2 × 2 summary of emotion regulation strategies

	Internal	*External*
Dysfunctional	Reject emotion Denial Depersonalisation	Bullying Hitting Shouting Vandalism
Functional	Learn from emotion Reappraisal	Talking to others Share feelings Writing blogs?

demonstrated. The combination of these two dimensions leads to the 2 × 2 classification system illustrated in Table 4.4.

We have given examples so far of the combinations of functional internal and external strategies and of dysfunctional internal strategies, but Table 4.4 also shows a fourth combination – that of dysfunctional *external* strategies that we have not yet commented on. Again, given the fact that most emotions are generated and experienced in interpersonal situations, there is no reason why the use of external interpersonal strategies should always be functional. Indeed, aggression towards others can be used by individuals to regulate a range of emotion states (DiGiuseppe & Tafrate, 2007) which may be dysfunctional for all concerned. We therefore consider that several of the external interpersonal (e.g. bullying, physical and verbal aggression) and other external strategies (e.g. aggression against inanimate objects) are also potentially dysfunctional, especially when used habitually (Phillips & Power, 2007). The details of how these strategies and other aspects of emotion should be assessed are presented in the next section.

Meta-Emotional Skills

In the last section, we presented information about meta-emotional skills both directly and indirectly, for example, when talking about the Regulation of Emotions Questionnaire (REQ). As with other regulatory processes, many emotion regulatory skills operate at an automatic level whether or not they fall into the 'functional' or 'dysfunctional' categories in the REQ. However, one of the clear meta-level skills is that reflective consciousness can be directed at our own lower-level emotional functioning and draw conclusions and set goals and plans for future emotional functioning. Indeed, much of the work of therapy can be seen as the development of such meta-emotional skills and enhancement of the role of reflective consciousness in daily functioning (Power, 2007). In order to be systematic about meta-emotional skills, we use different systems and levels within our own SPAARS approach, presented in Chapters 1 and 2, to provide a framework in which to consider such skills.

The analogical system

Low-level sensory and motor systems constitute the analogical system. This system may therefore seem an unlikely part of meta-emotional skills, but we argue that part of meta-emotional skill is to identify low-level sensory and motor problems in such systems and then to take whatever actions are appropriate to begin making slow changes in these systems. By analogy with sports skills, a professional tennis player might identify problems with his or her backhand that leads to problems during competitive play. The player will then need to re-learn the backhand by putting a new set of elements together under conscious control, until these become automatic and the backhand is improved.

The converse of this re-learning of a sports skill is the conscious interruption of the automatic functioning of a skill with periods of conscious control which may actually be disruptive to optimal performance, as when one starts to think about walking whilst walking. Analogical system sensory and motor skills relevant to emotion are the equivalent of such motor skills; for example, if a therapist is fine-tuned to detect micro-expressions of emotion, this skill can offer powerful insights into therapy sessions, but if the therapist ignores, or is not aware of, such fleeting expressions of emotion, these skills can and should be learned, as detailed later in the chapter.

Another example of an analogically linked meta-emotional skill is the awareness in oneself of these internal low-level reactions that are indicative of emotion and, equally, awareness of one's own facial micro-expressions, the physiological and behavioural signals that communicate our emotion states to others. For example, a micro-expression of disgust by a therapist working with a depressed client who is hypersensitive to criticism, and which the therapist then denies, is more than likely to lead to problems in the therapeutic relationship than if the therapist is, first, aware of the micro-expression and, second, able to turn the automatic reaction into an acknowledged issue that might be helpful to work on with the client. In summary therefore, we argue very strongly that therapists need to be aware of analogical system reactions in themselves and in their clients. Fleeting facial expressions of emotion known as micro-expressions are a very important example and we believe that all therapists should be trained in their detection (see Appendix 1 for details).

The associative system

Problems in the associative system share many similarities with the analogical system issues that we have outlined, because the associative system mostly operates at an automatic and effortless level outside awareness. The system embodies initial temperamental differences observable in babies (Kagan, 1994) that in interaction with attachment figures come to define different aspects of personality and emotionality. The development of reflective consciousness and meta-emotional skills again offers the individual an opportunity to make some changes to the functioning of this system. To cite a clinical example, a child with an anxious temperament became fearful of dogs from an early age and then subsequently became phobic. As a young adult, the person realized that the dog phobia could become an unnecessary restriction on her life, so she purchased a self-help book written by Rachman and de Silva (1996) and worked through her own graded exposure hierarchy. Now she runs a shelter for homeless dogs.

Unlike the example just cited, many people come to avoid those objects, situations and feelings that they experience as aversive. Such cognitive and behavioural avoidance, as we know from the earlier two-factor learning theories of anxiety (Rachman, 1990), inevitably make the avoided situation or feelings worse because there is no opportunity to learn that the feared outcomes do not occur. This argument does not imply that all avoidance is unhealthy, as noted earlier; some situations are genuinely dangerous, and individuals might avoid rock climbing or swimming out of their depth because such situations pose risk. However, if a situation arose in which they needed to climb a cliff to escape from an even greater danger, they would know how to make themselves feel as relaxed as possible and increase their chances of a successful escape, irrespective of their associative-level reactions.

The propositional system

Within SPAARS, the propositional system does not directly generate emotion (in contrast to Beck's cognitive therapy approach), but generates emotion either via the schematic model system or the associative route. Nevertheless, the propositional system plays an important role in the generation of emotion, as several subsequent examples will attest to.

One of the important developments in social cognition has been the concept of implicit (versus explicit) attitudes (Wittenbrink & Schwarz, 2007). In terms of the SPAARS framework, implicit attitudes could be represented as stored propositional representations, or at least be directly mappable onto such propositional representations. Such implicit attitudes may represent aspects of prejudice and stereotyping about other people on the basis of race, sex, gender, age or whatever and may directly conflict with an individual's explicit attitudes of tolerance, respect and equality. So what part do meta-emotional skills play in this system? First, there is the importance of awareness that such implicit attitudes exist within us and that they may conflict with our preferred explicit attitudes. One aspect of meta-emotional skills may therefore be to compensate for and be aware of these implicit prejudices and work to gain experiences opposite to the implicit attitude such as by having people of a different race or ethnic group as part of our social network.

Implicit attitudes are also likely to instantiate cultural views about emotion experience and emotion expression, the 'boys don't cry'-type problem. If therapists are unaware of their own implicit attitudes, for example about gender and emotion, during therapy, they may unconsciously guide men away from fear and sadness and women away from anger. These implicit attitudes may contradict explicitly held beliefs about the importance of all emotions for both sexes, and thereby may create a conflict in the client about whether or not such emotions are acceptable. Many clients come to therapy asking for problematic emotions such as anxiety and sadness to be removed and hold the mistaken view that some emotions are 'weak' and 'irrational', whereas other emotions are 'strong' and 'good'. These propositionally expressible beliefs about emotions may well become the focus of therapy, as later chapters spell out in detail.

We will also include the problem of the mislabelling or absence of labelling for emotion states as a propositional-level problem, because the label represents a proposition of the form 'This state is called anxiety' or whatever. An area that has received considerable attention has been that of 'alexithymia' (Taylor et al., 1997) in which individuals lack the label for emotion states even though they may experience those states. A basic meta-emotional skill that most children learn during development is the labels for different emotion states together with rules of expression and regulation of those states. In working with people with intellectual disabilities, it has become increasingly common to assess such knowledge of emotion states and to include emotion training as appropriate (Baron-Cohen, 2004). However, as Taylor et al. (1997) have shown, there are many people of normal intellectual ability who also lack such emotion knowledge, so this knowledge should be assessed when there is any concern that clients struggle during discussion of their own or others' emotion states.

A brief comment is also made in this section about the use of swear words to express emotions. The words and phrases used for swearing have a clear propositional structure in addition to their immediate emotional expression and impact. In fact, swear words provide an interesting example of how frequently repeated propositional material automatically evokes emotion via the associative route. Any language or culture can create such 'taboo' words; in Western cultures swearing historically involved blaspheming against God whilst the Church was more politically powerful during the Middle Ages (as in 'blimey' from 'god blind me!' or 'zounds' from 'god's wounds!'), but today certain body functions and parts are more generally used as swear words (Allan & Burridge, 2006). Although the expression used is often only a single word, typically there is an implicit propositional structure with an implied subject and object, which is why we include them under the rubric of 'propositional'. Swearing is typically used to express intensity or suddenness of emotion or to evoke an emotional reaction in someone else, but the meta-emotional skill is in knowing the 'rules of usage', for example how its use indicates status or intimacy in a relationship (Allan & Burridge, 2006). The overuse of swearing can be seen as excessively aggressive and inappropriate and its reduction may need to be part of an anger management intervention. However, it can also be indicative of other problems, as in coprophilia in Tourette's syndrome or a loss of the capacity to inhibit swearing in some neurodegenerative conditions (Jay, 2000).

The schematic model system

The schematic model system is the most obvious system in which to see the operation of meta-emotional skills. This system has overall executive control of the experience, expression and regulation of emotion as these skills develop (or fail to develop) across the lifespan. The development of meta-emotional skills continues throughout adulthood and provides a major component of 'wisdom' in older adults. The conscious and effortful appraisal system on which emotion generated via dynamically created schematic models depends must incorporate a range of intrapersonal and interpersonal information that at its height appears creative and insightful, even blessed with divine inspiration, but at its worst seems idiosyncratic, perverse and highly dysfunctional. This highest level of integration can therefore range from being humiliatingly wrong to being inspirationally correct, and that is why we need to spend so much time talking about our emotions, and the events that cause our emotions, with other people. However, rather than remain at this abstract level of discussion, we provide a few specific examples that testify to the potential breadth of this system.

As a first example consider the difference between so-called 'instrumental' and 'reactive' aggression (Blair et al., 2005). Both types of aggression are typically (though not always) consequent on feeling angry, with 'reactive' aggression being the automatic and immediate 'kicking out', whereas 'instrumental' aggression includes the choice and decision that it would be advantageous to be aggressive at this point with this person. Of course, whether or not such instrumental aggression is used for good or bad is another issue (Blair et al., 2005), but the point here is that there is high-level control of the expression in which individuals judge that it is to their benefit to express anger in this way.

A second example of the use of a meta-emotional skill is the capacity to suppress the expression of an emotion in a situation because it would be inappropriate or disadvantageous to express it, yet to be able to express the emotion in a more appropriate context later. In the psychodynamic literature this skill is referred to as 'suppression', in contrast to the unconscious operation of 'repression' which becomes problematic when used habitually; thus, the classic longitudinal work of Vaillant (1990) considered earlier has shown that suppression contributes to longevity of life, whereas repression does not. The important point again is that, as with instrumental aggression, suppression requires a subtle form of executive control that is protective for the individual experiencing the emotion without the emotion being over- or under-regulated.

The interpersonal context

Most emotions occur in interpersonal contexts or involve the recollection of an interpersonal context. When we conducted workshops on emotion and asked participants to complete emotion diaries, almost all reported a recent interpersonal episode no matter what type of emotion was involved. The exceptions to this generalization have been the few people reporting getting angry with inanimate objects, for example the participant who lost her tether with her computer and started shouting at it and hitting it; interestingly, unlike most other anger episodes, this participant was glad she had got angry and felt better afterwards, especially given that the computer had started working better as well!

A major issue about the interpersonal context for emotion and emotion-focused therapy therefore has to do with the individual's social support and social network. One of the great strengths of the interpersonal psychotherapy approach developed by Myrna Weissman and her colleagues (Weissman et al., 2000) is the use of the so-called interpersonal inventory. This inventory can be completed relatively informally in a single assessment session in which all current and significant past relationships are reviewed with the client. However, we prefer to adapt the method more formally through the incorporation of a traditional social network analysis, combined with a more detailed analysis of social support from significant others using the Significant Others Scale (SOS) (Power et al., 1988). This assessment is presented in detail later in the chapter. However, from the meta-emotional skills point of view, one or two key areas to focus on as part of the interpersonal inventory assessment include an assessment of how well the client understands the emotional impact that key others have on him or her and, as a consequence, how the client manages, or indeed mismanages, those relationships. For example if a depressed client reports that his mother is highly critical of him and he feels pulled back every time he takes a step forward, but he allows her to have complete control over the amount and type of contact she has with him, then the client is failing to use meta-emotional and interpersonal skills for the management of an unhealthy relationship. In contrast, if this same client has a good friend to talk to and feels better on doing so but avoids the friend when depressed to avoid making the friend feel upset (despite what the friend says to the contrary), there is an equivalent failure in the opposite direction in using meta-emotional and interpersonal skills to manage this relationship. Meta-emotional and other interpersonal skills should be used to maximize contact with healthy members of the social network, but carefully manage and minimize contact with the emotionally difficult or damaging members of that network.

One final specific point made in this section is that telling lies and the capacity to detect lying in others are two sides of an interesting set of meta-emotional interpersonal skills. The capacity to lie is a major milestone in child development in that the child must hold at least two schematic models simultaneously – one that represents the information to be hidden and the other that represents the false situation to be presented. The child must therefore possess theory of mind skills, which take account of the consequences of the other knowing the truthful information in comparison to the preferable consequences if the other believes the false information. Of course, children are not very good liars (Talwar et al., 2007), and there tends to be 'leakage' of the truth, such as the 'I didn't eat the chocolate ice cream!' claim made while being covered in chocolate ice cream. Adults are more skilled at lying, but studies of facial expressions show leakage for most adults also; for example, when smiles are used to mask more negative feelings, there are typically micro-expressions of sadness, disgust, anger or anxiety during the smile, and there is less involvement of the muscles around the eyes in the mask smile (Ekman et al., 2005). Whilst the capacity to lie and deceive may yet again appear to be a more negative meta-emotional skill, on the positive side some individuals are particularly skilled at detecting lying in others and appear to be tuned into non-verbal expression especially facial micro-expressions (Ekman & O'Sullivan, 1991). Our belief is that all therapists should be trained in these facial micro-expression analyses, as we spell out in detail later in this chapter (see also Appendix 1).

Measures of Emotion and Emotion Regulation

Measures of symptoms

Hundreds of measures of the range of emotions, stress, symptoms, emotion regulation and coping strategies are of course available that are clinically informative for a thorough assessment of clients' presenting with problems. We have already been critical of some of these measures earlier in the chapter either because they are tied into atheoretical classification systems or because they conceptualize an area such as depression poorly or incorrectly. To make a generalization, the simpler the concept being measured, usually the better the measure. For example, measures of anxiety tend to do exactly what they say on the label, and generic measures such as the Beck Anxiety Inventory (BAI) (Beck et al., 1988), the Spielberger State Trait Anxiety Inventory (STAI) (Spielberger, 1983) and the anxiety subscale of the Hospital Anxiety and Depression Scale (HADS) (Zigmond & Snaith, 1983) are extremely useful for assessment. They can be accompanied by more specific assessments of phobias, social anxiety, health anxiety or whatever, as appropriate.

In contrast, measures of more complex concepts such as depression tend to have obvious weaknesses such as the focus on guilt rather than shame and the poor coverage of interpersonal problems noted earlier for the BDI. However, this limitation on the BDI is relatively minor compared to the deficits on the HADS. The depression subscale for the HADS covers anhedonia well (four of the seven items cover some aspect of anhedonia), but it fails to ask anything about sadness or guilt and certainly does not ask about shame or even suicidality. By any account, the HADS depression subscale is appalling and should never be used to assess depression again. It makes the BDI look like the Rolls Royce of self-report measures. Because of the problems outlined with commonly used measures of depression, such as the BDI and the HADS, we have now developed our own measure of depression, the so-called New Multidimensional Depression Scale (NMDS) (Power

& Cheung, in preparation). The NMDS has four subscales that cover items for cognitive, emotion, somatic and interpersonal domains, with its particular advantages being that it covers the interpersonal domain appropriately and that it assesses shame as well as guilt. The latest version of the scale, which is still in development, is presented in Appendix 2.

In part because of the complexity of depression as a concept, widely used semi-structured interviews can be administered by trained clinicians and clinical researchers. The most widely used of these is the Hamilton Depression Rating Scale (HDRS) in its original 17-item format (Hamilton, 1960). The measure gives too much weight to sleep problems and, like the BDI, focuses on guilt rather than shame. However, the actual wording for guilt probably incorporates implicit aspects of shame through the mention of sinfulness and punishment, with the highest scores including delusions and accusatory hallucinations. It seems likely therefore that clinicians and researchers will have included shame and guilt together in their ratings on this item, so in practice the measure may work better than it appears to on paper. Therefore for the assessment of depression, clinicians should be trained in the use of the HDRS.

Self-report measures of emotions

In contrast to the full-scale industry for the measurement of stress and symptoms, a more modest industry has developed scales for the measurement of emotion. We argued previously against the use of Watson et al.'s (1988) PANAS on the grounds that it contains a number of non-emotion items, that it covers the range of basic emotions very poorly and that the two-dimensional theory of affect (the proposal that positive and negative affect dimensions are orthogonal to each other) is disputed even by other dimensional affect theorists (Russell & Carroll, 1999).

The Differential Emotions Scale (DES) is one based on the idea of basic emotions (Izard et al., 1993). It has been used in emotion research but seldom in clinical research or clinical assessment. The scale consists of 36 items, with 11 scales for discrete emotions and 1 for inner-directed hostility. The discrete emotions are enjoyment, interest, surprise, anger, contempt, disgust, fear, guilt, sadness, shame and shyness. It is unclear why interest and surprise are included as discrete emotions, and they are of little use to assess for clinical purposes; we would also derive guilt and shame from disgust, shyness as a type of fear and contempt as anger coupled with disgust (Power & Dalgleish, 2008).

For these and other reasons, we therefore developed the BES (Power, 2006). The measure consists of 20 items rated on the seven-point Likert scale (from 'not at all' to 'all of the time') (see Appendix 3). The items are grouped into five subscales that measure anger, sadness, fear, disgust and happiness; that is, the five basic emotions that we and others have previously argued form the core set of all basic emotions (Oatley & Johnson-Laird, 1987; Power & Dalgleish, 1997, 2008). We believe that the scale provides revealing clinical information that other scales do not offer, especially with the coverage of emotions across the whole emotion domain. In addition to our use of the scale in research (Power & Tarsia, 2007), we routinely use it in clinical assessment because it frequently detects issues with emotions that have not been reported as part of the initial referral or that might not be systematically examined in a clinical interview.

We have also developed the REQ (Phillips & Power, 2007), which, as noted earlier, offers insights into the client's routine use of different emotion regulation strategies grouped into four main categories: internal–functional, internal–dysfunctional, external–functional and external–dysfunctional (see Appendix 4). Again, we believe that in addition to the use of scale in research, it offers extremely valuable clinical insights that provide a wealth of material for the emotion focus in therapy.

There are many other self-report measures in the broad area of emotion, though they may be of less use clinically. One example is the area of so-called EI, in which a number of self-report and performance-based measures have been developed. We (Power & Dalgleish, 2008) believe that the label 'intelligence' is a mistake and provides the wrong elitist message about emotional skills. We have proposed the term 'meta-emotional skills' instead and believe that the concept of a skill is preferable to that of intelligence because it avoids many of the trait implications of the latter. Nevertheless, many self-report and performance-based measures have either been developed as part of the EI concept or have become linked to it even though they were not originally developed as part of it. One such useful measure is the Toronto Alexithymia Scale (TAS-20) (Taylor et al., 1997), which is a self-report measure that focuses on whether or not respondents can identify and describe their feelings ('alexithymia' literally means 'without the words for emotions'). In addition, Taylor and others (e.g. Taylor, 2001) have found an excessive external focus and a poor fantasy life in such individuals, and the TAS-20 includes an external focus scale. A broader self-report scale of EI is Bar-On's (1997) Emotional Quotient Inventory (EQ-i) which includes 12 subscales, some of which such as empathy, emotional self-awareness and impulse control are useful. However, many of the subscales stray well into areas of self-esteem, extroversion and assertiveness that lose whatever value there is in trying to identify EI as a separate concept. We are currently developing a 'Meta-Emotional Skills' (MES) questionnaire that goes beyond our REQ and draws directly on the SPAARS model and the different skills that are necessary to function optimally at the different levels.

Finally this section notes the importance of emotion diaries that can be used by clients in between therapy sessions as and when key emotions occur during the week. The single-page three- and five-column versions of such diaries are widely used in cognitive therapy (see Figure 4.1), and they can provide a useful summary and session-to-session reminder of distressing experiences for the client. The use of a diary in itself can offer a possible means of coping and resolving difficult issues and emotions, as we know from the work of Pennebaker (1982).

We also like to use the more detailed Emotion Diary shown in Appendix 5 and adapted from Oatley and Duncan (1992). Although developed as a research tool, we find that especially near the beginning of therapy, data provided at the time of an emotion is much more informative than that obtained with the single-page three- and five-column versions. The Emotion Diary, for example, begins to identify other emotions that may be concomitants or that may be coupled with the primary emotion, it assesses the extent to which the person tries to avoid or inhibit the emotion, and it can help clients tune in better to their emotional experiences.

Performance-based measures of emotion

We have taken the traditional focus in this chapter on the use of self-report measures given to clients, but, as we have also hinted

Situation	Thoughts	Feelings

Figure 4.1 An example of a three-column diary

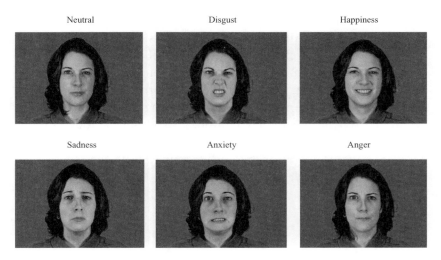

Figure 4.2   Facial expressions for neutral and five basic emotions

at, we believe that therapists should receive formal training in the identification of clients' emotional expressions.

A set of the basic emotion faces is presented in Figure 4.2. We assume that all therapists can easily identify the five basic emotions of anger, disgust, fear, sadness and happiness that these faces illustrate, so you may well ask what is there to learn about facial expression? Why do I need training? The need for training arises because we believe that all therapists should become experts at detecting the fleeting expressions of emotion, the micro-expressions that might only last for a fraction of a second and whose presence might often be masked with smiles, an averted face or a hand covering the mouth. Although Ekman et al. (2005) have developed training especially for use in forensic and similar settings in which individuals may attempt to deceive deliberately, the confusion and uncertainty over feelings that clinical clients often experience provide invaluable clues for therapy. Therapists have therefore missed the opportunity to become experts in these micro-expressions, and we recommend that therapists add this skill to their armamentarium (see Appendix 1 for details).

In addition to facial expression, there is a range of other non-verbal and physiological clues to which most therapists have paid little formal attention. Again, therapists may believe that learning these is necessary only in forensic settings when trying to detect deception. However, we believe that training in deception detection is also useful in tuning therapists into these aspects of non-verbal expression in their clients. Although most therapists neither have access to nor want to use multichannel polygraphs in their work, many rarely comment on the often-visible external signs of changes in physiology such as blushing, other reddening, sweating, breathing rate, twitching and restlessness. In sum, we are not proposing that therapy sessions be carried out in expensively equipped psychophysiology laboratories, but that expertise in the use of facial and non-verbal analyses becomes a requirement for therapist training rather than being seen as interesting but irrelevant.

5
Too Much Emotion

They are insane who try
To reach that point, and those that go beyond
Are torn by anguish
—Anna Akhmatova

Many clients come to therapy in the hope that the therapist will remove an unwanted or overwhelming emotion; that the therapist will possess some magical surgical technique by which the aversive feelings of anxiety, or depression, or such, can be removed, and they can be left in a permanent state of calm happiness. Of course, such requests are not as wild as they might appear, given that there is a pharmaceutical industry that claims such miracles for its products. And, indeed, most of the clients that eventually attend for psychological therapies will have tried at least one, if not many, of the pharmaceutical industry's magic cures. Some clients may even have found moderate benefit from some of the medication that they have tried. Our purpose is not to launch an attack on the pharmaceutical industry but merely to bring some reality into people's expectations.

John was a thirtysomething office worker who described himself as normally a calm and unemotional person. Recently he had begun having overwhelming feelings of anxiety, which left him sweating and feeling like he was suffocating while at work. He had managed to hide these episodes from his colleagues in the open plan office in which he worked by rushing off to the toilet and locking himself in there until the feelings passed. However, he was now worried that his colleagues would eventually notice and that the feelings would get so bad that he would be unable to come out of the toilet. He had visited his GP and been given some medication, but the medication had given him unpleasant side effects and he had stopped taking it. His main request was that the awful feelings should be taken away so that he could get back to being his normal calm self again.

For many of the emotional disorders, clients present to therapy stating, like John, that they experience *too much emotion*. In some cases the therapist may well agree, for example, in case of overwhelming grief following the loss of a loved one and in which the client's life is completely disrupted by constant feelings of sadness and other emotions. The agreed aim with such cases may well be to help the client bring their feelings back under some sense of manageability though without getting rid of the feelings altogether. In other cases such as John's, there may be a contrasting concern that the client's normal emotional level is excessively over-inhibited and that the experience of any unpleasant emotion is set against a background in which no emotion is acceptable. We examine certain extreme types of these cases in detail in the next chapter when we consider *too little emotion*. Nevertheless, we need to be mindful that the experience of *too much* can either be because there is genuinely too much or because there is normally too little emotion.

We examine each of the basic emotions of fear, sadness, anger, disgust and happiness with case examples of each. Before doing so, we consider several common issues or problems that arise across the different emotions and their disorders.

1. The emotion is experienced as overwhelming but is not present for most of the time. The panic attack is the classic example of this category in that they may be experienced very infrequently, but because of a range of avoidance strategies, they may nevertheless be completely disruptive of the person's life. The actual experience of the emotion is, however, what is crucial; thus, the person may think that he or she is dying, is going mad, will damage self or others and will do something embarrassing or humiliating as part of the loss of control.

2. There may be cultural and religious influences in addition to family ones for the experience or expression of certain emotions. The classic Western cultural pressures that we have already mentioned include the tradition that men should not experience 'weak feminine' emotions such as fear and sadness and that women should not experience or express 'strong masculine' emotions such as anger. However, there are many other cultural and religious influences, for example, the ambivalence of Catholicism towards sexuality and the even more extreme attempts by some Calvinist groups to eliminate pleasure. Clients from such religious backgrounds may be overwhelmed by constant feelings of guilt and shame because of their preoccupations with forbidden sinful pleasures, which from other ideological perspectives are perfectly natural and normal.

3. The sense of 'loss of self' during the emotion. If part of the child's socialization has been to eliminate the experience and expression of a particular emotion, the child never learns to experience such an emotion as part of the developing self-concept. If and when the emotion is experienced therefore, the emotion state is ego-dystonic; that is, the emotion is experienced in a 'not-self' manner and clients may report such feelings as derealization and depersonalization during the emotion. For example, a woman who as a child was socialized to eliminate any feelings of anger may come to experience states of anger as if she were being taken over by someone else that is not herself. Such an experience of loss of self can be extremely terrifying when it occurs in this way.

4. Emotion switching is a common problem with emotions that are socialized out because they are disallowed. For example, apparent problems with anger and aggression in men can be a result of feelings of anxiety or sadness which are not allowed but in which the anger and aggression take away the weak and unacceptable feeling and replace it with a more acceptable feeling. Similarly, in women socialized not to experience anger, there may be a switch into distress and apparent sadness when the initial appraisal has led to anger. These emotion switches have a clear function for the individual but often lead to problems with referral because the person is referred for the wrong problem. Detailed examples are given later in the chapter.

5. The chronic presence of an emotion. As noted above, there are some emotion and mood states that are present chronically and

the individual typically becomes worn down and fatigued by the emotion or mood state. For example, the chronic worrier who never feels free of anxiety, the person with severe depression who is bed-ridden for months or the obsessive–compulsive person who lives with a constant sense of contamination and for whom extensive rituals barely give any relief. Many of the problems that we deal with in therapy are about chronic emotion or mood states. Within the SPAARS approach, we have identified several factors that contribute to such chronic states, including, as outlined in Chapter 2, the coupling of different emotions (e.g. sadness and anger in some chronic grief states), the impact of beliefs about emotions (e.g. avoiding talking to friends when depressed because it will make the friends upset) and the 'modularization' of the self-concept (e.g. in the bipolar disorders, in which emotion states lead to excessively positive or excessively negative self-states that are more difficult to regulate).

Each of these factors is illustrated with clinical cases in the remaining sections of the chapter, with us examining too much emotion in relation to fear, sadness, anger, disgust and happiness.

Too Much Fear

There are two extremes in the anxiety disorders and plenty of combinations somewhere in between. At one extreme is the single experience of a panic attack, which may be attributed to a particular object or situation, which then leads to continuous cognitive and behavioural avoidance. At the other extreme are the chronic worriers or generalized anxiety disorder sufferers, the agoraphobic clients who dare not leave the house (at least not alone) and the posttraumatic stress disorder (PTSD) sufferers who are in a permanent state of hypervigilance and hyperarousal out of fear of further trauma.

Panic attacks are a common experience in the population, with the evidence suggesting that more than 40% of individuals report the experience of such attacks (Rachman, 2004). Only a small proportion of people who experience panic attacks seek help. We know from David Clark's (1986) work that of those seeking help, most misattribute the panic attack to indicate a catastrophic outcome such as a heart attack, a brain haemorrhage or a feeling of losing control and going mad. Two key aspects of cognitive therapy are therefore education about what panic attacks are and helping the individual to apply this new schematic model during the actual experience of a panic attack.

At this point it is worth noting that the initial behavioural work on the treatment of phobias from Joseph Wolpe (e.g. 1958) onwards emphasized the importance of the activation of the anxiety state so that the individual worked through that state, whether in imagination as in Wolpe's systematic desensitization procedures, or in graded exposure *in vivo* in later developments (Marks, 1969). Granted we would no longer subscribe to the old-fashioned behavioural principles on which Wolpe based therapeutic change, nevertheless, the shift to more talk and less emotion in the cognitive therapies has paradoxically led to *less* rather than *more* use of working with emotions directly in modern-day approaches: too much talk and not enough emotion.

The behavioural use of repeated emotion arousal in dealing with low base-rate avoided emotions such as panic is therefore correct in principle, especially when combined with education about the emotion and training in the use of emotion-regulation strategies other than avoidance. The main aim of emotion-focused cognitive therapy (EFCT) is to help the person be able to experience the emotion whilst having the ego resources to hold the experience in awareness without the self being overwhelmed and with a realistic schematic model or understanding of what the experience is about. However, in contrast to David Clark, we would not attribute all panic attacks simply to incorrect schematic models ('catastrophic misinterpretations' in Clark's terms). Many panic attacks do not have their origin in the catastrophic misinterpretations of bodily symptoms but are described as arising spontaneously by people experiencing them. Night terrors are an example of such 'spontaneous' or non-schematic model generation of panic, but within the SPAARS approach, these occur through the generation of panic attacks via the automatic route.

Hamish had recently left the army because he had begun to have night terrors but felt too ashamed to seek help while still serving. He had worked in an undercover capacity in many different conflicts and war zones because he had always thought of himself as 'tougher' than those around him. If anything got to him, he drank, and drank until he got over it. That approach had worked for most of his time in the army, but a couple of years ago he had started waking up with night terrors. He had many repeating dreams primarily from his time in Northern Ireland where he had worked undercover. One dream was of an incident in which he should have been travelling in one particular car but some colleagues had instead. They were blown up and he found the body parts of his friends and colleagues scattered around the landscape. Sometimes it is this dream, at other times there are other equally gruesome dreams, but at times he wakes up in a panic without recalling any preceding dream. His normal way of handling such experiences using drink and drugs was now getting out of hand and so he had developed problem drinking in addition to everything else. He always kept a bottle of whisky at his bedside and would immediately begin drinking if he woke up with a night terror.

Part of the problem for Hamish was of course that he had been socialized into rejecting anxiety as an unacceptable weak feminine emotion and, indeed, had spent almost all his adult life in an army culture that had strongly reinforced such a view of anxiety to the extent that he had to leave the army rather than own up to feeling such shameful emotions. As is common in exposure work with PTSD sufferers (Richards et al, 1994), we made some audiotapes of three of the worst repeating dreams so that we could work with Hamish both in session and during the day to help him experience panic attacks whilst awake and without resorting to alcohol or drugs to ameliorate the effects. Initially, he became aggressive because of not being allowed to use his normal emotion regulation strategies but with persistent repeated experience of anxiety and panic he came to see that it was even more courageous to allow himself to experience something than it was to run away from it. Courage whilst experiencing fear rather than simply avoiding it, eventually gave Hamish a greater sense of accomplishment and a more realistic view of the range of acceptable emotions for even a man such as himself. Indeed, Hamish gained a renewed confidence in himself to the extent that, and I would agree with those who might see this as an inadvertently poor outcome of therapy, that he became a mercenary soldier and has since appeared in more African and other conflicts than one would care to mention.

Although exposure in imagination and *in vivo* may well be useful in low-rate acute phenomena like panic attacks, in chronic disorders the person is in the emotion or mood state much of the time and a different challenge is presented for therapy. Chronic worry and chronic anxiety states are classic examples in which exposure-based approaches are simply not relevant and initial behavioural techniques such as applied relaxation can often exacerbate rather than improve the problem. However, ideas such as from Tom Borkovec and colleagues (e.g. Borkovec & Roehmer, 1995) fit very well into the SPAARS framework and provide an interesting EFCT application to such states; that is, the possibility that the constant worrying about relatively minor issues may in fact act as a defence or a way of inhibiting much more major worries that occur at an associative or automatic level. The aim of therapy therefore is to pare away the outer layers of the more trivial worries to get to the underlying major worries. We are not claiming that this model applies invariably to chronic worry, because, as noted more abstractly at the beginning of this chapter, there may be many factors that can contribute to chronic states. However, we believe that it is necessary to examine this possibility in the treatment of chronic worry and generalized anxiety because it is relevant for at least some, in the same way that Freud's notion of retroflective anger is relevant for some depressions but is discredited as a general theory of depression (Power & Dalgleish, 2008).

Euan was in such a chronic state of worry and anxiety that the therapy session lengths were increased to two hours because it was not possible to do any therapeutic work in less time. Because of his anxieties, one of which was forgetting or missing something that was important both in therapy and in life, Euan spent all his time taking down notes in all situations to such an extent that it was difficult to get into some of the rooms in his flat because of the boxes of notes he had stored there. Euan was referred initially because he was training in medicine and surgery and had failed some of his Royal College membership exams. He therefore wanted help with exam revision methods. The problems turned out to be far more complex than exam anxiety and revision methods, though the focus on these for the first part of therapy and his success with his retaken exams then allowed Euan to develop a good working relationship in which, after a break, he returned to therapy and we were able to work on more fundamental issues. To summarize his background, Euan had been adopted at birth into a prestigious family, and his adoptive father was a famous surgeon. Euan had never felt worthy of his family, always feeling as if he were on trial and that if he did not do well enough he would be abandoned again. It transpired that he hated surgery as a specialty, though there were some aspects of medicine that he seemed to enjoy especially the idea of teaching general medicine. Interestingly, his father apparently despised the 'teaching' role and only valued the 'doing' role, but handling his father's initial contemptuous reactions as Euan worked out what he wanted for himself rather than what his father might approve of was crucial for Euan's progress. Indeed, by the end of therapy, the sessions had reduced to one hour, and Euan's occasional impulse to write something down was easily challenged and he began to laugh at himself rather than feel anxious.

In Euan's case therefore there was a very complex underlying conflict that the constant state of more superficial worries seemed to help him avoid. However, only after dealing with the immediate set of worries (exams he had failed once) was it possible to establish a therapeutic relationship in which the underlying issues became amenable to exploration. To have simply gone straight in and attacked Euan's note-taking and other strategies for dealing with his anxiety could have led to premature termination of therapy and a therapeutic failure for the reasons outlined in Chapter 3. Only after therapy moved onto the underlying issue of the relationship between Euan and his father were occasional comments about note-taking dealt with constructively. In particular, when he would interrupt the flow of the session on feeling something strongly and start writing notes, the feeding back of exactly that sequence – of using note-taking to cope with a strong feeling towards his father – slowly began to help him to stay with painful feelings rather than immediately attempt to rid himself of them. Euan's self- and emotional-development had been significantly distorted by his adoptive status and his fear that he would be abandoned unless he did what his father wanted. Although Euan was correct in believing that his father's reaction to him standing up to him would be one of contempt, and indeed the father was equally, from Euan's accounts, contemptuous of our therapeutic work, in the longer term, his father came to respect him for his own choices. Their relationship began to become an adult one, in which he now related directly to his father, whereas previously he always related to his father through his mother. In fact, Euan's father apparently even became less contemptuous of 'those damned psychologists' who 'always blame the parents'!

Too Much Sadness

The problems related to sadness tend to be associated with more chronic conditions such as depression and problematic grief reactions, but even within such chronic conditions, acute but rare overwhelming feelings of sadness can occur for which the person can seek help.

> Lawrence was a sixtysomething Glaswegian who had come from a tough working-class family in which men definitely did not cry. He recalled bursting into tears at age six because he had been bullied at primary school and being beaten by his grandfather for it and being forced to attend boxing lessons for many years which ensured that he was never bullied again. Unfortunately, his wife, who had been his first love as a teenager, had died two years before and subsequently Lawrence had experienced occasional uncontrollable episodes of crying and an intense pain that he had never known before. He thought he was going mad because he felt so out of control at these times of grief. His grown-up children had now banned him from seeing both them and his grandchildren because he became very aggressive at these times and had gotten into fights with two of his sons-in-law.

Lawrence, it turned out, used the emotion-switching strategy of becoming angry and aggressive when other people were around, and he wanted to disguise how he was really feeling. However, he was fully aware that it was the sudden and overwhelming feelings of sadness that were his main problem. Indeed, Lawrence's feelings of 'going mad' during these times was very similar to the descriptions given by panic clients who sometimes present with the feeling of 'going mad' as well. That is, the intense emotion, whether panic or sadness, is so unacceptable to and so disavowed by the self that the person feels that the self is lost when the emotion predominates.

Initial attempts to work with Lawrence's feelings of sadness in sessions were greeted with intense shame and strong aggressiveness in an attempt to force me to back off. Lawrence likened me to his grandfather in that despite my protestations to the contrary, he thought that I 'really' saw him as weak and inadequate when he felt like crying. On several initial occasions he ran out of the room because he felt so ashamed of the fact that he was about to cry, though on each occasion he returned after 15 minutes or so extremely embarrassed by what he had done. His initial reactions were that I would stop seeing him in therapy because his behaviour in therapy was so unacceptable, or so he believed.

The most significant point of change in therapy with Lawrence was when for the first time he allowed himself to cry in front of me without running out of the room. As with the client who allows himself to feel anxious, it is important to keep the person in the unwanted emotion state without trying to reject the emotion state and from there to help make the feeling state become more familiar, less aversive and more owned by the person. As Lawrence began to appreciate that I did not see sadness as a feeling to be ashamed of but a feeling that is perfectly natural and one that takes courage to experience, sadness became more acceptable to him and the feelings of going mad diminished.

Although Lawrence is presented here as an example of acute problems in the experience of an occasional but overwhelming emotion, he also illustrates many important aspects of a chronic state of so-called atypical or chronic grief. As Lawrence explained, he had lost his first and only love and his best friend. There was no way he wanted to be in any future relationship because, two years after her death, he still missed his wife as intensely as the day that she had died. Lawrence had built a memorial for her in their house with photographs and belongings such as hair brushes, scarves and jewellery that she had especially liked. He kept all her clothes, and every night he slept in her nightdress because it made him feel closer to her. He was strongly religious, though his wife's death had left him feeling angry with god for taking her away from him. Nevertheless, his religious beliefs had stopped him from taking his own life even though he sometimes knew that was all he wanted to do to rejoin his wife. He spoke regularly with his wife and heard her voice speaking back to him especially in certain parts of the house such as where he had built the memorial to her.

In dealing with long-term chronic grief such as Lawrence's, therapists can be forgiven if they turn to the research on grief about what is the best way to deal with such problems, yet come away feeling confused! From the work of John Bowlby (1969) onwards, there seemed to be a clear view that there was a series of stages of grief that the mourner needed to work through to finally let go of the lost person. However, more recent research has questioned the inevitability of such stages, it has suggested that poorer outcomes result from getting people to express sadness and other 'negative' emotions and that the notion of 'letting-go' might be an unnecessary and even inappropriate goal for some losses (Stroebe et al., 2001). Although such large-scale studies and their group or 'averaged' statistics should always be treated extremely cautiously when working clinically with a particular individual, there are one or two pointers in the current research that highlight some necessary cautions for clinical work with grief. In Lawrence's case, the group statistics stating that it is wrong to explore or to encourage 'negative' emotions in mourning is simply completely misleading. Lawrence demonstrates the need to make an individual formulation rather than mindlessly apply such 'evidence-based' nonsense. No group statistics will highlight the individual plight of a Glaswegian working-class male such as Lawrence, socialized into believing that the ultimate weakness was to feel sadness, and how he was convinced that he was going mad because at the age of 60 he had been overwhelmed by such feelings for the first time since he was six years old. In therapy, it was absolutely necessary to help Lawrence experience sadness but without feeling shame or feeling that he was descending into madness. However, the recent research was correct in Lawrence's case to suggest that the aim of letting-go of the lost person sometimes may not be an appropriate one. Lawrence's strong religious beliefs and certainty that his wife awaited him in the afterlife, together with the significance of his wife to him from his teenage years on, meant that 'letting go' was not a therapeutic aim. Instead, the therapeutic aim became how to get more out of his remaining time in this life because his wife would not have wanted him to suffer so much on her behalf and that she would still have wanted him to have companionship and be engaged in life in a meaningful way. So instead of letting go of her, he began working in a shelter for the homeless, people whom he saw as worse off than himself, that was run by nuns. He also went back to his local church and began talking to the priest, who had known him for many years, about his anger with god and, eventually, Lawrence began to participate again in church activities.

Perhaps the commonest disorder that might be expected under *too much sadness* is that of depression as well as grief following in the tradition from Freud's (1917) *Mourning and Melancholia* that linked the two together. There is no dispute that sadness is an important component of depression. In a recent empirical analysis of emotions present in depression (Power & Tarsia, 2007), we showed that the general scales of sadness and disgust were important contributions to depression severity scores in a clinical sample, though when we looked at specific emotions, 'gloominess' (or 'misery') together with 'shame' made the most significant contributions. Although 'gloominess' is an emotion primarily derived from sadness, it also has a slightly different quality that includes a hopelessness about the future in addition to pure sadness. For these reasons therefore, we will delay a consideration of depression until the later section in this chapter in which we consider *too much disgust*.

Too Much Anger

The over-inhibition of anger can be accompanied by rare outbursts of too much anger (DiGuiseppe & Tafrate, 2007) in which, in extreme cases, individuals can carry out extreme acts of violence including murder. Although we are mindful of the fact that aggression does not only result from the emotion of anger (we have already presented cases in which aggression was associated with anxiety or with sadness), there is a high association between the two, which has to be taken into account in any anger management programme.

> Robert was described by his work colleagues, his friends and his family as an extremely quiet and emotionless person. He talked little, but when he did, he had a slow calm manner about him. He had been married for 12 years and had two daughters aged 6 and 8 years. He was always very calm with his daughters and had never been seen to get angry or to scold them. Nobody could believe it when they heard that late one night he had lost control and murdered his wife.

Robert had come from an extremely religious background and had been brought up never to be angry or aggressive but always 'to turn the other cheek'. That is exactly what Robert had managed for almost all his life, but he stated that his marriage had gradually deteriorated over the years and that he had come to feel at a distance and to feel misunderstood by his wife. She had dealt with his unhappiness and distance by getting increasingly angry with him and, he said, by constantly nagging him. Because of his religious beliefs, he said he felt trapped and unable to divorce his wife, though he knew that many others in the same situation would have done so. However, he had always managed to deal with his wife's nagging and criticising him until that fatal night when he could not explain what happened to him but it felt like 'someone else had taken him over'.

Robert had clearly described the problem we have seen with other emotions, which when socialized out from the developing child's acceptable experiences can lead to problems in both personal and interpersonal functioning later in life. Be it anger, sadness, anxiety or any other feeling, on the rare occasions when these rejected emotions are experienced, the person typically reports a loss of sense of self and a melodramatic set of consequences can result because they do not know how to express or regulate the emotion as they are experiencing it. Although the consequences of experiencing sadness and anxiety in such cases are rarely as extreme as in cases of anger such as Robert's, the same principles hold for therapy in that the individual needs to be helped to experience anger on a more regular basis so that it becomes both a familiar experience and one that the person learns to manage other than through acts of violence. In Robert's case, the intervention was carried out in a Special Hospital in which he was held indefinitely because of the risk he was considered to have for others. As part of a weekly anger management programme, Robert brought anger-related incidents from during the week, which were then role-played in group to explore his emotions and emotional experience. The group was run for a year, and over that time Robert showed an increase in self-reported experiences of anger that seemed to be better managed and that he reported feeling more 'part of him' than his rare previous experiences of anger.

Robert's case is fortunately an uncommon and extreme one, whereas the more typical problems with anger tend to be feeling angry too often, with hindsight often over trivial incidents, and feeling in a permanent state of irritability in which anger and aggression are always a short step away. Such states of irritability can accompany other problems such as depression or hypomania/mania, or they can simply be problems in their own right.

George said that he had always been somewhat uptight and 'on a short fuse' but that he had managed to control his temper for most of his life. That is, until a year ago when he had been rushing late for an appointment and while driving in this state he had a heart attack and crashed his car into a lamppost. A passing motorist who stopped turned out to be a physician, who realized that George was having a heart attack and resuscitated him. Had it not been for the physician, he said that he would definitely now be dead. Since then, every minute felt like it could be his last, so he felt angry at the most trivial things that got in his way or slowed him down, and he got angry with anybody who disagreed with him or questioned him. His wife had moved back to living with her parents, and his friends had started avoiding him.

In George's case, therefore, anger felt like an all-too familiar or ego-syntonic experience, with too much anger and constant irritability having turned someone with a short fuse into an always-exploding time bomb. Although George partly believed that each moment could be his last, there was a conflict in that he now wanted life to be perfect and full of success and happiness. He was far from resigned to wanting the next minute to be his last, yet his behaviour was making another heart attack more rather than less likely.

The EFCT intervention with George focused therefore on the maelstrom of emotions that converged into his feeling that he was living each minute as if it were his last, therefore anything that got in the way of his enjoying that last minute got trampled. The existential problem that was at the forefront of George's awareness is in fact a possibility that all of us have to live with if we dare to stop and think about it – the next minute could be our last. But unless you are standing in front of a firing squad, it is very rarely that we know that the next minute actually will be our last. And even in front of a firing squad you cannot be absolutely sure, as the Russian novelist Fyodor Dostoevsky found with a last-minute reprieve when standing in front of a firing squad. George's experience of a heart attack brought him into full awareness of the proximity of death, yet, as we suggest, every time you cross a busy road you could be a fraction of a second away from mutilation or death. However, one gets on with life without ruminating how close to death we were whilst crossing that last road. The existential problem for George meant that the possibility of death was not to be challenged (in contrast to working with panic attacks in David Clark's cognitive therapy model) but to be accepted in the way that our mortality is implicitly accepted in everything we normally do. George therefore was helped to accept the possibility of death in this existential sense, to reduce how much this schematic model fuelled his anger and aggression.

The next step in George's treatment was how to regulate his feelings of anger and aggression and express them in a more appropriate way, along the lines recommended by Aristotle:

> Anyone can get angry – that is easy; ... but to do this to the right person, to the right extent, at the right time, with the right motive, and in the right way, that is not for everyone nor is it easy; wherefore goodness is both rare and laudable and noble (Aristotle, 1947).
> Reproduced from Aristotle (1947). *Nicomachean Ethics* [W.D. Ross trans] In R. McKeon (Ed), Modern Library, New York.

First of all, George's existential acceptance led to him becoming less angry less often. Nevertheless, there was still an issue about him continuing to evaluate a situation, even if it was making him angry, about whether he should suppress the anger, whether it would be appropriate to express the anger and if it was appropriate to express it, what form would be most effective. We used both his in-session and between-session experiences of anger to experiment with and learn from. He was also interested in the evidence on the so-called Type A personality, which now seems to indicate that either too much or too little anger increases the risk of cardiac problems, in contrast to the earlier evidence that it was only too much anger that increased the risk. So George was well motivated to learn about the appropriate regulation and expression of his anger.

Too Much Disgust

Two different types of disgust reactions are considered in this section. First, the classic obsessive–compulsive reaction, which, although traditionally described as an anxiety disorder, is, according to us, sometimes disgust based rather than anxiety based (Power & Dalgleish, 1997). The second type of disorder we consider here is depression. Although as noted earlier, depression also has sadness as a component emotion, we think that it is the self-disgust component, particularly shame, that turns mere sadness into depression (Power & Dalgleish, 1997; Power & Tarsia, 2007). Our first example, however, is that of OCD.

> Brian was a 28-year-old man who lived with his mother. Brian felt he was in a permanent state of 'contamination' – that the world was a dirty and disease-ridden place and that any contact he had with it outside of his flat meant that he would have to rush home and spend hours showering until the feeling of contamination was removed. Because the outside world felt so contaminating, he went outside as seldom as possible. He had given up his work in an office several years ago and his mother would normally go shopping for both of them and deal with outside activities. He had a girlfriend some years ago, but she had left him when his problems had become more noticeable. Although he now spent almost all of his time in his flat, he found that even his mother opening a door or window, or someone coming into the flat was now beginning to make him feel contaminated. On the rare occasions he had to go out, he was unable to use a public toilet so he would have to get home in time because of the problems this caused.

Brian was unable to articulate clearly what he meant by 'feeling contaminated', but it seemed to be a disgust reaction that any of us would feel, he said, as if you had gone to the toilet and got faeces on your hands – 'Wouldn't you want to wash your hands immediately if that's what had happened to you?'

The standard behavioural or cognitive behavioural intervention for problems such as Brian's is exposure plus response prevention (Rachman, 2003). This behavioural approach is correct in its aim to evoke the unwanted emotional state in the client, but it is simplistic and incorrect in its view of why change occurs. In classical behavioural theory, the view is that repeated exposure plus response prevention leads to extinction of the classically conditioned emotional response. Such an aim is unnecessary. In an EFCT approach, the aim is to help the client learn about the emotion state, learn how to tolerate the emotion, learn how to accept it, learn that it is possible to distract oneself from the state and learn how to use other methods to downregulate the experience. Only to aim for the extinction of the emotional reaction would be both naïve and simplistic. In Brian's case therefore we worked to give him a broad range of skills to deal with the feeling of contamination – how to hold and accept the presence of the feeling, how to distract himself from the feeling and how to talk himself down from the feeling. Rather than completely preventing the compulsion of showering, we agreed to limit the number of times and duration of time during the day that he would shower, so that eventually he was limited to one shower for a maximum of 15 minutes per day.

One of the things avoided with Brian was getting into 'intellectual battles' over notions of germs, degree of contamination of the outside world, likelihood of catching a disease and so on, contrary to the 'challenges' that would be used in a standard cognitive therapy approach (Salkovskis, 1985). Such cognitive challenges can remain forever stuck at an abstract level that never connects with the crucial emotion state in which patterns of thinking and reasoning may become quite different from those present in a neutral intellectual state. In a sense, the approach with Brian was similar to that taken with George, discussed in the previous section on anger, in which it was agreed that every minute could be our last, but that was an existential truth for everybody. Rather than get locked into arguments with Brian about probability levels of possible contamination both inside and outside the home, we agreed that there was such a probability, and that whether this was one-in-ten, one-in-a-hundred or one-in-a-thousand was not going to make much difference to how he felt and what he wanted to do when he had a feeling of contamination. The starting point therefore was the feeling and how he experienced that feeling, rather than the thinking and the probability estimates.

In the next example, we spend some time considering the problem of depression. As explained earlier, we have argued that depression typically involves the coupling of emotions such as sadness with disgust, though high levels of anxiety and anger can also be present (Power & Dalgleish, 2008). The disgust focus in depression is primarily on the self rather than on the whole range of potential disgust-related objects, though there is some mixed evidence that other types of disgust may also be elevated (Rozin et al., 1999). When disgust is focused on the self, then typical disgust-related emotions include shame and guilt, with shame being seen as a reaction towards the self as a whole, and guilt being a reaction typically to actions carried out by the self. Shame therefore is the emotion with the greater pathogenic qualities in that the whole self is seen to be wanting and, indeed, we have found it to be more significant than guilt in clinical depression (Power & Tarsia, 2007).

How does disgust and subsequently shame come to be focused on the self? First of all, it is easy to identify certain cultural and religious factors that may take aspects of the self to be disgusting in some way. For example, Christian views on sin and original sin imply that the person must fight against sinful aspects of the self and overcome them; thus, sex, greed, avarice, pride and so on can be treated as sinful, and disgust-based reactions are socialized into the child during development over such characteristics. An interesting prediction on these grounds is that some religions should be associated with higher levels of depression than others; for example, relevant findings from a European epidemiological study suggest that at least amongst older adults, depression rates are higher in Protestant than in Catholic countries (Braam et al, 2001).

In addition to religious and cultural influences on the development of self-disgust, there are strong familial influences. Disgust-based socialization is a more important factor than has previously been recognized, not only in relation to potty training but in relation to a wide range of socially prescribed ways of relating. Of particular interest to EFCT is the fact that because emotions arise primarily in interpersonal relationships, they are typically about the rights and wrongs that relate to significant interactions. If a significant other hurts you, do you have the right to get angry with that person and seek apology and retribution? Or are you expected to swallow your anger because you neither have the right to be angry nor to make demands on a significant other? If you work hard but fail to pass an important exam, what view does this leave you of yourself, what emotions do you feel towards yourself and what emotions do you think others have towards you?

> Wyn had been brought up in a strictly religious household in which only her father had been allowed to get angry and even then that primarily occurred when he would come home drunk. Her parents had a cold and unsupportive relationship in which her mother nevertheless tried to be the 'perfect wife' and keep the peace. Wyn described her first marriage as very similar; she had felt 'unreal' but had tried to be the perfectly dressed trophy wife for her businessman husband. She felt totally devastated therefore when she found out that her husband had been having an affair for over a year, so she walked out of the marriage. Wyn was now in a new relationship in which she felt like a real person, but she sometimes found herself overwhelmed with periods of anger for which she then became completely ashamed and felt loathsome, and she was convinced that her new partner would leave her if she continued getting angry with him.

The therapeutic focus with Wyn therefore was that on the one hand there was a genuine step forward that she was now both feeling angry and being angry and that *constructive* anger was a good and necessary aspect of every relationship. Wyn's concern however was that her anger was *destructive* and so part of the work was trying to disentangle what aspects of her anger came from the backlog of unresolved feelings towards her parents and towards her ex-husband and what aspects of her anger genuinely arose in her new relationship. Part of the process of therapy was therefore to see if Wyn could now express her anger towards her mother (her father had died some years previously) and towards her ex-husband. Her first attempt at getting angry with her mother turned into a disaster in that her mother refused to see her again and threatened to cut her out of her will. We were therefore able to consider where her views about *destructive* anger originated from and that, in relation to her mother, Wyn had learned as a child that any expression of anger would have destructive consequences. Unfortunately, however, there were later destructive consequences for her in adulthood of not getting angry and not being able to resolve interpersonal issues in a constructive manner.

Wyn therefore presented with a complex coupling of emotions that constituted her depression. She felt sad at the loss of her marriage, at the loss of her father without being able to resolve these issues with him and at the constant conviction that her current relationship was about to end. She felt angry for the reasons her marriage had gone wrong, with her parents for the way they had treated her, and with her current partner for her belief that he was going to leave her. And she felt utterly ashamed at herself for feeling all of these weak emotions, especially the unwanted anger which left her feeling humiliated after she had expressed it.

Too Much Happiness

When the pursuit of happiness seems to be everything, it may seem like a strange idea that one could have too much of a good thing. Unfortunately, the paucity of English terms and the overuse of the word 'happiness' means that we are not claiming that the long-term sense of fulfilment or satisfaction in life (Aristotle's 'eudaimonea') is a bad thing, but that there can be excesses of the short-term emotion of 'happiness' such as in elation in hypomanic and manic states and in drug-induced states, especially when these are coupled with other emotions such as anger or anxiety. Although as we have noted else-where (Power, 2006), manic states have typically been characterized as excesses of elation, in fact empirical investigation suggests that large numbers of manic episodes are characterized as much by dys-phoria as by elation, with the presence of high levels of anxiety and irritability. Hence, our analysis of manic states (Power & Dalgleish, 2008), which has now been incorporated into a new measure of mania and depression (Cavanagh et al., 2009), has focused on the coupling of anxiety and anger with elation, rather than on elation per se. The person who is in such a state is extremely difficult to work with using any type of intervention, in that when they become a risk to them-selves and others through their uncontrolled and grandiose actions, they may have to be legally detained and treated. One of the aims of the adapted interventions we have developed for working with people with bipolar disorders includes the recognition of early warning signs so that the person (and a carer) can take appropriate action at the very early stages of a manic episode before the episode runs out of control (Schwannauer & Power, in preparation; see also Lam et al, 1999).

> Irena was a fortysomething single woman who had experienced multiple episodes of mania and depression since her early twenties. Her first episode of mania had started just before her final exams at university and at the time she had used the high energy levels and need for very little sleep to get through the exam period. Unfortunately, subsequent manic episodes had not been so productive, and she had been arrested on many occasions for a variety of offences including wandering naked through the town centre, starting fights in bars (she had now been banned from most of the bars near where she lived) and possession of illegal drugs. An analysis of potential early warning signs showed three that she began to monitor on a daily basis because they seemed the most useful: the number of telephone calls she made (at the beginning of episodes, my Ansaphone would be filled with her calls); the amount of sleep that she needed and how irritable she felt with everyone (e.g. most of the telephone messages that she left would quickly turn irritable and aggressive). When all three of these early warning signs began heading in the same direction, Irena would contact one of the medical team for an immediate review of her situation to take fast and appropriate action.

It would be easy to fill this section on *too much happiness* with the details of numerous cases of mania and hypomania, but that would give the misleading impression that only these disorders of happiness existed. However, in the broader scheme of things, the misappropriate pursuit of happiness, in one or other of its various forms, can also lead to a range of physical and mental health problems. These milder variants are less likely to come in the way of the psychological therapist as primary presenting problems, but the issues are there hidden behind a range of other problems. We touched upon one such class of problems earlier when we considered people asking for their anxiety or depression or such to be taken away and replaced by happiness. Many more people than those we want to see in the clinic want to rid themselves of 'negative emotions' and replace these with only positive ones. Some of the referrals for 'somatization problems' and interpersonal skills problems are typically based on these misunderstandings about emotions and on poor tolerance of aversive negative emotional states.

In interpersonal psychotherapy (IPT) (Klerman et al., 1984), one of the so-called focus areas for therapy was originally that of 'interpersonal deficits' (it has now been renamed as 'sensitivities'). Clients with such 'deficits' tend to have very restricted social networks with no intimate or confiding relationships. Indeed, they are often puzzled about why other people are not nicer to them, but have a tendency to externalize the source of their problems. One of the ways of working in EFCT (and in IPT) with such cases is, once the therapeutic relationship has been well established, to begin to give feedback on the impact of the client on the therapist. For example, if the therapist is aware of always having to work too hard or always having to initiate interaction in the therapy sessions, that in itself needs to become the focus of the therapy, with the therapist commenting back to clients how they feel in therapy and attempting to link these feelings to how others might feel or might have felt in their interactions with them.

> Jane had no close friends even though she was studying as a postgraduate student and worked evenings in a bar. It was not therefore because of a lack of opportunity for meeting people but, rather, that she allowed herself to be drawn passively into unsuitable relationships, which she subsequently ended when they became clearly unsuitable. Her most recent relationships were with older men whom she had met through working in the bar, but she was now even more cynical about relationships because although she thought that they would be more interested in her when she had sex with them, in fact they seemed to be less interested after they had had sex. Jane reported that she felt off colour most of the time with a range of headaches, stomach aches and backaches, but that these experiences with men took her into feelings of depression. She had no female friends.

Jane's passivity was evident in therapy – she simply wanted therapy to make her happy, to stop her feeling depressed, and she sat silently in sessions waiting for this to happen.

> *Therapist*: I am aware that you normally sit waiting for me to start any conversations – that you don't spontaneously start them yourself.
> *Jane*: Do you think so? [thinks . . . silence] . . . Yeh, I guess you might be right.
> *Therapist*: What was happening then during the silence? How were you feeling?
> *Jane*: I feel worried about what you might be thinking about me . . .
> *Therapist*: And what do you imagine?
> *Jane*: That you feel bored with me . . . That nothing I say is of any interest to you . . .
> *Therapist*: But do you feel that staying silent and saying nothing would be more boring or less boring than saying something?

Jane: But what if you don't like what I say? What if I say something you disagree with?

Therapist: But maybe that's what relationships are all about – that they are about taking some risks and about letting people know about how you feel and how they make you feel.

Jane: That feels so scary! I always avoid talking about feelings to people.

Therapist: Then perhaps we could spend the rest of the session talking about how we feel about each other, because it would be good to try these things here first.

Jane: [laughs] . . . you mean I should actually tell you how I feel about you! That just sounds so difficult . . .

Therapist: Difficult but not impossible . . . like, how do you feel right now?

Jane: [laughs] . . . you know, I feel just a bit alive . . . So often I feel just dead inside, like nothing is happening . . . but now I feel just a small spark.

Therapist: But do you think you could tell me directly how you feel about me? Whether it was positive, or negative – or both positive and negative?

Jane: I would need to be sure that I can trust you, but I never felt that trust before . . . You know how my father left myself, my brother, and my mother when we were very young . . . My mother always felt at her limit coping with us so I learned to keep all my feelings to myself.

Therapist: But do you feel that I am like your mother? That I am working at my limits and would be unable to take anything that you were to throw at me?

Jane: Maybe not so far, but maybe I haven't really thrown anything at you yet!

Therapist: Ah, but those silences that up until now I have worked hard to break so as to try and engage you in therapy – they at times feel even more difficult than if you were to throw something more directly at me.

Jane: My mother used to seem relieved that I was silent and didn't make demands on her.

Therapist: But what was good for your mother, isn't right for me, it isn't the way you can get the most out of therapy, and it isn't the way you can get the most out of your relationships in your day-to-day-life.

Jane: Well, I will give it a try, at least in therapy . . . you know, I already feel a bit better about being here than I have up until now.

In Jane's case, she learned to be more open and honest in the therapeutic relationship about her feelings about herself and about the therapist. In turn, these gains helped to improve her day-to-day relationships. Although she never became the extrovert at the centre of attention, she began to bring herself more into relationships to learn more about whether those relationships were right for her. In particular, she became closer to one of her female classmates, and for the first time in her life, had a girlfriend to whom she became close.

Summary

In this chapter, we have tried to explore a range of clinical examples in which clients have experienced *too much emotion*. The examples have ranged across all of the basic emotions and included panic, worry, anger, disgust, sadness and happiness. Many people want less of the so-called negative emotions – they want to get rid of their anxiety, panic attacks or sadness – and they attend therapy with unrealistic views about their emotions. EFCT, like all therapies, therefore has to have an educational role in which clients increase their knowledge about emotions and what they are. However, knowledge is only one step; for many people it is also about learning to accept the experience of an emotion, or learning alternative strategies for emotion regulation in place of the dysfunctional strategies such as drugs, alcohol and behavioural avoidance that they may have used to date. For those clients who experience a chronic and persistent aversive emotional state, there is a need for a good individual formulation that, in particular, establishes the maintaining factors for the chronic presence of the mood and emotion states. In the example we considered of chronic grief, there seemed to be a cycle of sadness, anger and shame with no working-through of the actual loss; here, the function of therapy was to help the client accept sadness as neither strong nor weak, as neither masculine nor feminine but simply as a normal state that everybody experiences, especially following such a significant loss.

In the case of too much happiness, the story is typically very different. The problem is that many clients pursue too much 'happiness' at the detriment of themselves and their relationships, irrespective of whether that happiness is obtained through drug and alcohol 'highs', through risky activities or through dangerous liaisons. We live in cultures in which the pursuit of happiness appears to encourage such short-term hedonism, though in fact at least part of such encouragement comes from the overworked word 'happiness' itself having too many significant meanings in English.

6
Too Little Emotion

I regret nothing, neither do I complain nor weep . . .
My heart grows chill within
—Sergey Yesenin

There is such a force and historical tradition in our culture that men are rational and that women, being the weaker and more vulnerable sex, are emotional. What a story this tells us about the mess that our culture is in! The philosophy and psychology books should be torn up and thrown away because they tell us nothing – in fact, exactly what Descartes proposed when he wrote *The Passions of the Soul* in 1649! Unfortunately, whilst Descartes took a step forward in his presentation of the *passions,* he took a step backwards by giving us the mind–body split, which has further added to the emotional confusion that our culture finds itself in.

There are undoubtedly temperamental differences between infants at birth (Kagan, 1994), but all of us, men and women alike, start with the same set of basic emotions (Lewis, 2000). But it is clear that these basic emotions are subject to a wide variety of socialization influences from the very start. Who knows what effects dressing boys in blue and girls in pink right from birth have on their emotional development! More seriously, we know from studies such as that of

Barrett et al.'s (1993) that even by three or four years of age, there are major differences between boys and girls in their experiences of shame and guilt; that in reaction to the same event, girls by three or four years of age are more likely to experience the more debilitating emotion of shame, whereas boys are more likely to experience guilt.

A similar story is told if we look at the continuities and discontinuities from childhood to adulthood psychological disorders. Although boys and girls experience the same range and numbers of childhood fears and phobias, by adulthood women outnumber men in the experience of phobias, which often show continuity from childhood fears, whereas there is a much lower rate of continuity in men (Rutter, 1984). What is happening therefore that leads to similar rates of fear in boys and girls, but by adulthood women far outnumber men? The same problem arises with the rates for depression. In childhood boys and girls show approximately equal rates of depression, if anything, boys slight outnumber girls (Harrington, 2004). Beyond puberty however, the rates change and women show approximately twice the rate of depression as do men, the ratios varying somewhat with different cultures that reflect on the expected roles of adult women.

These few outline facts and figures point to the conclusion that our culture does not deal well with emotion. The key splits in our culture are the rational–emotional and mind–body splits, which provide the context in which the emotional disorders develop. In particular, the *genderization* of emotion has disastrous consequences. Boys don't cry, men don't feel fear, woman don't get angry. In this chapter therefore we again examine the five basic emotions of fear, sadness, anger, disgust and happiness and consider some of the consequences of experiencing or expressing too little of these emotions. Of course, as we pointed out in the last chapter, sometimes emotions can be experienced like the overrestraint-binge cycles that are found in the eating disorders, with people moving between extremes at times of too much emotion and too little emotion; such cycles tend to arise from the person's belief that he or she should not experience emotion because it is too overwhelming, but overinhibition is the source of the problem. Finally, given the mind–body split, we will also consider the links between the inhibition of emotion and the increased risk of different somatic disorders where appropriate.

Fear

We looked at the case of Lawrence in the previous chapter because, following his wife's early and unexpected death, he was overwhelmed by sadness. Yet Lawrence was still the stereotypical Glaswegian male who regularly drank too much and got into fights in bars.

> Lawrence at a young age told his grandfather, who was his main carer, that he was being bullied at school. The grandfather's reaction was to beat him until he promised never to feel afraid of anyone again and then sent him to boxing lessons, so that by his teenage years, he was an accomplished boxer with some local notoriety. Lawrence had met, fallen in love with and married his first girlfriend. She was everything for him – the mother who had gone out to work full-time and the devoted and caring wife. But when she died, not only was he overwhelmed with sadness he was also overwhelmed with a fear he described as being a vulnerable child again – an experience he simply did not know how to deal with. So like any stereotypical Glaswegian male, he would get a bellyfull of drink in him and fight any man who came near him.

Lawrence's problem was very clear to formulate: He had not been allowed to experience fear (or sadness) from an early age, but if he did ever experience these unacceptable feelings, he would resort to drinking, to alcohol, or to some private support that he obtained from his wife within the confines of their marriage. Lawrence had lost the main support in his life, and, because of his drinking and his aggression, his own adult children had also rejected him. The aims of therapy were therefore, first, to change Lawrence's schematic model of the unacceptability of fear and sadness. The schematic model was worked with through a combination of educational, challenge and experiential techniques, the overall aim of which was to help Lawrence allow these emotions into his experiential life without resorting to his habitual emotion regulation strategies. In effect, the educational and experiential strategies are designed to present the person with two schematic models which are in conflict with each other so that the person is aware that the two models conflict and that a resolution of these conflicting models is desirable and needs to be brought about. The first of these schematic models is the one that is typically the long-standing such as 'boys don't cry' in Lawrence's case, and the second model is the more recently constructed one along the lines of 'crying is a normal response to loss'.

> *Lawrence:* I feel frightened without Mary. She did so much for me . . . Sometimes she said I was like her biggest child . . . (Lawrence stands up to leave the room.)
>
> *Therapist:* Lawrence, I know you're feeling some very strong emotions right now and you don't want me to see them, but just tell me first what you think will happen if you stay?
>
> *Lawrence:* (still standing) . . . My grandfather told me never to be afraid. You're a man like him . . . you're gonna despise me and think I'm a stupid child for feeling so frightened and wanting to cry in front of you.
>
> *Therapist:* I know those were your grandfather's views, Lawrence. But I am not your grandfather. I think that men who can show how they really feel are stronger, not weaker. At least give me the chance to prove that to you – stay and sit down and see how it feels . . .
>
> *Lawrence:* (sitting down slowly) . . . I will try, I will try. But every time I feel afraid I can hear my grandfather telling me off, I can feel him hitting me around the face . . .
>
> *Therapist:* Well, that wasn't right of him Lawrence. I don't think he helped you by doing that – certainly not now when you have these over-whelming feelings of fear and sadness every day . . . I wonder if you could imagine just being able to experience these feelings without thinking they are good or bad. Why don't we try that now? . . . . Stop trying to get rid of the fear, stop thinking that it's bad and you shouldn't feel it. Just experience it, as if you were feeling hungry. . .
>
> *Lawrence:* (laughing) . . . That's gonna take some getting used to after all these years! But I will give it a try.

Lawrence did try very hard; hence, over the space of a few months, he discovered that allowing himself to feel fear and sadness actually gave him a sense of relief and periods of calm he had not experienced before. Although, as we noted in the previous chapter, he never let go of his wife, and we accepted that the grief work would not include that aim, he began drinking less, became closer to his children and grand-children again, and started volunteering in a religious community for the homeless.

The second example in this section on too little fear is that of so-called *repressors* and the repressive coping style. The usual analysis of this style is the avoidance of fear to maintain positive affect (Derakshan et al., 2008), though it remains unanswered whether repressors also avoid other emotions such as anger, disgust and sadness that can also be aversive. Our clinical suspicion is that the problem ranges beyond the avoidance of anxiety, but we await some proper empirical research to answer this question. Although the term originates with Freud in his book with Josef Breuer *Studies on Hysteria* (1895), he used it in a wide variety of ways throughout his writings. More recently, there have been attempts to operationalize the concept as someone who scores very low on measures of anxiety, but very high on measures of defensiveness or social desirability (Weinberger et al., 1979). Weinberger et al. (1979) and other recent research have demonstrated that repressors report low anxiety, but unlike genuinely low anxious individuals, they demonstrate high levels of distress on a range of physiological (e.g. heart rate, skin resistance or forehead tension) and behavioural (e.g. reaction times, avoidance or verbal interference) indices. The fact that repressors are physiologically and behaviourally aroused is of particular concern for physical health and a variety of somatic conditions, and, indeed, repressors have been found to be at increased risk for several disorders, including circulatory disorders and cancer.

> Lily was a 70-year old woman referred to psychology services following a range of physical health–related screens, which failed to reveal any physical source for the headaches, fatigue and other aches and pains that she had begun to experience. She was puzzled about her GP having referred her to a psychologist, because all psychologists did was talk about your childhood, and she had had a very happy childhood. When asked about any recent changes in her life, she said that her husband had died a couple of years ago, but 'You have to look on the bright side of life, don't you?' It was a shame, she said, that she had experienced all these headaches and other pains since, and now her blood pressure was dangerously high and her GP was worried about her so, to keep him happy, she thought she would come and see me, because she was sure she might need him for other things in the future. On completion of an anxiety scale, Lily scored in the low range and commented, 'I don't like to get anxious – it's not good for you is it?!'

Clearly numerous problems were worked on in therapy with Lily, in particular the problematic grief reaction. However, Lily's bereavement had occurred in someone who had a repressive coping style, which then broke down to some extent with the experience of a severe life event but which was also leading to a range of relatively minor somatic complaints that had the potential to become more serious.

Assuming that repressors are made and not born, it is nevertheless difficult to overcome a lifetime of automated habit. In Lily's case, the first step in therapy was to provide her with information and education about the links between avoidance of emotion and the occurrence of somatic problems such as headaches, dizziness and fatigue. Intellectually, therefore, she began to accept that there might be such a link – that, using the old pressure analogy, if you bottle something up, it may come out in other ways if too much pressure builds up in the system. Now this analogy draws on the basic Freudian thermodynamic principle that mental energy gets converted into symptoms (Power, 1997), but this principle only has a partial truth under extreme circumstances such as Lily's and can also be accounted for by other mechanisms (Power & Dalgleish, 2008).

The next stage in Lily's therapy, once she had accepted intellectually that there was a link between her emotion avoidance and her physical symptoms, was to help her to find out for herself that if she allowed herself to experience these difficult emotions such as anxiety, anger and sadness, which her physical symptomatology reduced, but if she bottled up her emotions, her physical symptomatology was likely to increase. Of course, the mapping is not quite so clear-cut and immediate as the equation might suggest, so we got Lily to carry out daily monitoring of headaches, fatigue and blood pressure (with a small portable sphygmomanometer) on days when she either talked to her daughter (who lived with her and who was her main confidante) about her fears and concerns, or on other days when the daughter was out late, or Lily only talked to her about other things but not how she felt. This fairly crude experiment proved very effective with Lily, because we could both see a pattern that emerged from her daily monitoring that, contrary to her original view that talking about bad things made you feel worse, in fact in they began to make her feel better. Even after we stopped the experiment, our follow-up meetings showed that there were times when Lily slipped back into her old pattern of emotional avoidance; however, she now took note of her headaches and feelings of fatigue as warning signs she was most probably avoiding dealing with her emotions.

The third example in this section comes from the area of post-traumatic stress disorder (PTSD). As Tim Dalgleish and I, together with a number of others, have summarized (Dalgleish & Power, 2004; Janoff-Bulman, 1992), the two routes to emotion generation within the SPAARS model provide important features of different types of

PTSD. On the one hand, PTSD is characterized by low-level analogical system phenomena such as vivid intrusive memories of the sights, sounds and smells of the traumatic event. However, some types of PTSD also provide challenges at the schematic model level in that significant beliefs about the self and the world can be 'shattered' by the traumatic event, such as when a person's beliefs about safety and invulnerability are challenged by a driving accident. For the detailed example considered later in the chapter, we turn back to the Glaswegian man as an example of how invulnerability beliefs can be challenged and lead to PTSD.

> Jimmy was known as the hard man amongst his friends. He worked as a bouncer in a nightclub, and occasionally participated in other activities that he was somewhat vague about. He lived on a council estate on the outskirts of Glasgow, where, he said, you needed to be tough just to survive. He believed that emotion was for women, children and wimps from Edinburgh. Unfortunately, however, one night when walking back somewhat drunk from the nightclub to his flat, he got into a fight with a group of teenagers, who stole his wallet and put him into hospital for nearly a week because of broken ribs. He still felt in pain and experienced flashbacks of the experience. But what was even worse, he said, was that he felt like being in a constant state of fear and anxiety and was too afraid to step out of his flat. He had therefore given up his job as a bouncer. Much to his shame, he was also suffering from impotence, and his wife was now jeering him about this.

Jimmy had believed that he was invulnerable and was the toughest guy on the block no one dared to challenge. However, in the end it was a group of what he called children, which demolished this view and, in the process, left him overwhelmed by fear and shame. Although there were also some low-level intrusive features of his PTSD, the formulation primarily focused on his prior beliefs of invulnerability together with his rejection of 'weak emotions' such as fear. Instead of using an exposure-based treatment therefore, the focus was on exploring the beliefs, their origins and consequences, along with helping him to experience anxiety as a normal emotion without feeling ashamed of it. Eventually, Jimmy came to see that his previous beliefs about himself and the world were extremely unrealistic. He also discovered a 'softer' side to himself that helped him spend more time with his children and had now begun to coach his son's school football team. Jimmy reported that his wife and children seemed even to prefer the 'new Jimmy' because he was much more accessible and pleasanter to live with.

Sadness

Grief following the loss of a loved one provides the greatest challenge for people who have problems with the experience and expression of sadness. In our culture, such problems are often very common in men, as in the case of Lawrence already mentioned, though often the presenting problem can be something other than grief such as drink and aggression problems because of the unacceptability of sadness for such individuals.

> Dave had lost his partner of 12 years six months before he was referred for help. He had worked as a freelance computer expert and had been very busy six or seven days a week up until the time of his partner's sudden death in a road accident. Since that time, however, he described himself as living in a trance – he felt nothing, but he could do nothing and his diary was now completely blank, when just until six months before, it had been full. Dave now lived alone and, he said, he had been unable even to remove his partner's, Sandra's, clothes from the clotheshorse where they were still hanging to dry, or to remove her makeup from the dressing-table in his room. He had felt nothing from the time that she had died.

Dave had completely numbed his inner experience in a way that he reported not thinking or feeling anything as if he were asleep with his eyes open. The goals in therapy were therefore very clear – to help Dave begin to experience his emotions and to begin the process of grieving for his partner, however painful such feelings were going to be. One of the significant precursors for Dave's own reaction had been that his mother had died from cancer when he was a teenager, but after her death, his father simply stopped functioning and became almost zombielike, in Dave's description of him. So Dave's father had also dealt with his painful emotions by cutting himself off from his feelings and from those around him, and now Dave was doing the same. The breakthrough for Dave came indirectly in therapy through dealing with the issues about whether he could ever be with another woman because that would mean being disloyal to Sandra. He acknowledged that had he been the one to have died, he would not have wanted her to put herself through what he was going through but would rather that she had found someone else for her to be with. He started dating someone who had known them both and who had tried to be supportive following Sandra's death, but he had pushed her away. His new girlfriend was very supportive and a natural therapist; Dave found opening up emotionally to her easier than he could in front of me, a male therapist, so my main function was to act as a catalyst for the therapy and recovery that his new girlfriend was able to provide him with.

One of the issues that we have been aware of from our clinical work with both unipolar depression and with bipolar disorders is that during recovery some individuals attempt to keep their range of emotional experience too narrow and too restricted and that everyday variations in mood and emotion generate anxiety that they are heading towards a relapse. This problem has been most apparent through the work we have done with bipolar disorders because of the use of daily monitoring of key signs as part of the intervention.

Donald was a 30-year-old man who had suffered from a bipolar disorder from the age of 18, though he had not been properly diagnosed until he was in his mid-20s. During therapy, we established a set of four warning signs that he monitored daily. His partner also monitored the same signs and they discussed any issues or concerns that arose. The key warning signs for Donald included hours of sleep, energy level, aches or pains and feelings of anxiety. However, as we continued monitoring anxiety levels through his recovery and a period of health, it became apparent that he had not only little tolerance for any feelings of anxiety but even more so for feelings of sadness. Any such feelings were interpreted to mean that he was about to relapse, but we were able to work together to use the monitoring form to broaden the permissible range of emotional experience, especially when the other signs, such as sleep and energy levels, being monitored remained at his normal level.

Of course, it is unclear in cases such as Donald's whether his attempts to keep his emotional experience within a very narrow range were a cause or a consequence of his episodes of mania and depression. But working with him in this way decreased the number of hospitalizations and improved his general sense of well-being.

Anger

In the previous chapter we considered the example of an emotionally overcontrolled man who expressed almost no emotion, but who then murdered his wife. Such an example highlights the potential disastrous consequences of an extreme of too little of an emotion, which then leads to the opposite, the excessive expression of that emotion. However, rather than focus on such dramatic examples that are so well-known to our forensic colleagues, we use a much more mundane example from clinical practice of the inability to experience and express anger.

> Kate had married when both she and her husband were in their teenage years, but now, some 25 years later, the marriage seemed to have stagnated, though Kate seemed unsure why. At the time of their marriage, she had worked as a secretary, but because her husband's work had required him to move around the country every few years, she had given up work and stayed at home, where she had a very large garden that took up all her time and energy. Although about 10 years previously they had decided to have children, unfortunately Kate had miscarried and found the experience too distressing to want to take such a risk again. Kate now presented with low-level chronic depression that had been ongoing for long enough to place her in the dysthymic disorder category. She stated that she never got angry.

One of the key issues that came up in working with Kate was the fact that she spent much of her time on her own because her husband was now away from home on a weekly basis. When asked how she felt about this, she simply reported not feeling anything. She said that because she had been unable to have children that her husband had the right to go away on business as often as he needed to and she had no right to challenge him or to express any opinion about his absences. However, what had prompted her to see her GP and ask for help was the fact that for the past year she had been having increasingly disturbing nightmares in which she dreamt that her husband was injured, maimed or even killed. She would wake up in a state of fear and, although to begin with she had managed to calm herself down, she had recently become so terrified by these repeating dreams that she woke up believing that her husband had actually been injured or killed. She had therefore begun phoning her husband at all hours of the day and night to check that he was OK. At first, he had humoured her and tried to laugh off her fears, but now he had started switching off his phone because he was getting so annoyed with her for waking him up in the middle of the night, or phoning him while he was in meetings.

At this point the alert reader might well ask what on earth do dreams of death and injury have to do with problems in the expression of anger? Of course, the psychoanalyst would smile knowingly and point to dreams being the royal road to the unconscious; that dreams have a latent content and wish-fulfilment function that converted the unacceptable aggression towards her husband into a reaction formation in which she becomes overcaring in case something might have happened to him. Also, because she is unable to locate the hostility towards her husband in herself, it becomes the world that has become too dangerous in a projection of her hostility onto objects and people outside of herself. There may well be much truth in such a proposed process, though the answer within the SPAARS model is far simpler – that anger is an unacceptable emotion for Kate at a conscious level – but in her case, her dreams and fantasies are simply one way in which her unconscious emotions are expressed. There were also other ways in which Kate expressed her anger without being aware that she was doing so, which included certain facial microexpressions and her use of silence at times when she might have been angry.

However, within the confines of a short-term therapy (we met for a total of 10 sessions), Kate was never able to access consciously any feelings of anger, and she simply looked at me in bemusement at the times when I tried to suggest that maybe these dreams were an expression of angry feelings in herself about her husband's absences and about the state of her marriage. In Kate's case, short-term therapy never helped her to connect with her anger, but we did help her to manage the nightmares better, to stop phoning her husband all of the time to check on his well-being and to look at additional ways in which to make her life feel more meaningful.

Now again, the cognitive behaviourist who has been brought up on an overdose of the Eysenckian phobia of Freud and any men-tion of the unconscious, may wish to dismiss the possibility that dreams, symptoms or parapraxes might be clues to unconscious emo-tions, and that any therapist who insists on their presence when the client denies their existence must be deluded. Well, such a cognitive behaviourist stands accused of simply being ignorant, for it is not only psychoanalysis that talks about processes that occur outside of the awareness of the individual but all areas of cognitive science and social psychology necessitate such unconscious processes. For example, in the work in Chapter 2 that we considered on social cognition, it is clearly necessary to consider both explicit attitudes and implicit or unconscious attitudes; we know from other work in social perception, self-deception and social judgment, such as in the classic work by Nisbett and Wilson (1977), that people are very poor interlocutors of their own reasoning and judgment processes. In Kate's case, it may well have been worth videoing her and identifying certain facial expressions and her use of silence to help her identify her expressions of anger to see if that would have helped her begin to recognize angry feelings in herself at the time. In Kate's case, the psychoanalyst might also point out that she is an example of Freud's (1917) formulation of depression in which anger is turned against the self. Our response has been that some forms of depression may well reflect such a process but that this does not provide a general model of depression (Power & Dalgleish, 2008); the unacceptability of emotions other than anger may also contribute to some types of depression, for example, the unacceptability of emotions such as fear and sadness in men.

Although we curtail our examples of anger at this point, we also note that anger and problems with its expression can also be a significant component in other disorders. In Chapter 7, a detailed example of a case of bulimia is presented in which problems with anger expression are also a significant component.

Disgust

The first images for the idea of too little disgust might include things like babies playing with their faeces, homeless individuals searching through dustbins and Norwegians eating whale meat. Such lack of basic disgust reactions can be seen in some clinical conditions such as Huntington's chorea (Gray et al., 1997) in which self-care skills may deteriorate as a consequence of the disorder. However, our reactions to food choices, for example, such as whether or not to eat whale meat, frog's legs or raw fish reflect the role of disgust in socialization in different cultures about what is acceptable and unacceptable rather than the lack of a disgust reaction.

A different type of disgust-based problem can emerge in some forms of psychopathology such as PTSD. We have seen several cases of emergency workers in which they have developed PTSD with the primary emotion being disgust rather than anxiety (Dalgleish & Power, 2004). The tasks that emergency workers must carry out frequently require them to be in situations that most people would react to with extreme nausea and disgust. For example, attending traffic accident victims, fires, assaults, murders and suicides exposes emergency workers to mutilation and destruction of the body that many of us never see in a lifetime (except perhaps now in B-grade horror films, which increasingly present gore and physical mutilation).

> Paul was a policeman who had been the first on the scene of a suicide. A middle-aged man had hanged himself in the deep cellar of his house, but his wife, who had just found him, had assumed that he had left with the woman he was having an affair with and had no idea that he might have killed himself until she walked into the cellar some weeks after he had disappeared. When Paul arrived on the scene, he found the wife in great distress and overwhelmed by guilt that she had not known that her husband's affair had finished and that he had felt so desperate because of it. What Paul saw, when he went into the cellar was a heavily decomposed body covered with flies and maggots and a stench that made him throw up on the spot. He felt completely ashamed of vomiting in front of the woman and now had constant flashbacks of the corpse covered in flies and maggots hanging from the ceiling.

In therapy, Paul reported that he was shocked at his reaction. He had attended many serious injuries and deaths and was even proud of the fact that he was able to stay calm and detached, when many of his colleagues had sometimes become overwhelmed. He felt bad now that he had often been contemptuous towards other police officers who had not handled such situations well. In terms of the SPAARS approach to PTSD therefore, Paul had both low-level intrusive phenomena (the sight and smell of the corpse and the nausea as he vomited) and high-level schematic model issues (being ashamed of his reaction in front of the woman and his colleagues getting back at him). The main work of therapy was to help Paul to understand that disgust reactions are perfectly normal healthy reactions that everybody has, but because his father had also been a policeman and dismissive of any weaknesses in him, he had somehow managed to overinhibit such reactions in himself for fear of reprisals. As part of therapy, he went back to see the woman and to see what she had thought about him for vomiting. In fact, she said that she had also vomited at the time and had been having problems with images of her husband's dead body ever since. Paul ended up talking to her for several hours; she told him that she had found his vomiting completely normal and nothing to be ashamed of given that she had reacted in exactly the same way; and both felt a sense of relief from having been open with each other about how they had been feeling. Paul subsequently returned to work. Although his colleagues initially continued to jibe him, he has now persuaded his seniors to establish occasional sessions for his unit on how to handle stressful situations.

Problems with too little disgust also arise with the complex emotions of shame and guilt, which we derive from the basic emotion of disgust (Power & Dalgleish, 2008).

The idea of too little guilt or too little shame immediately raises the spectre of the anti-social personality disorders in which some individuals are capable of carrying out actions that the rest of us would feel appalled by. Of course, a social psychologist such as Philip Zimbardo would argue that all of us have the potential to act in such ways, as *The Lucifer Effect: How Good People Turn Evil,* the title of his latest book conveys vividly (Zimbardo, 2007). The point we are making is that our shame and guilt reactions help to prevent us from carrying out such appalling actions, even if under extreme social circumstances and in certain roles, the majority of us might not be held back by those shame or guilt reactions. Our concern here is with those individuals who even under normal circumstances lack the inhibitions of shame and guilt, which in combination with poor empathy, can lead to considerable problems.

Gill was a lecturer in engineering in a large university department. She had recently been made redundant by her university following many years of disputes, including one in which she had accused two senior male professors in the department of sexual harassment and discrimination against her. She had also complained to their professional body. However, none of the complaints had been upheld and eventually the university failed to renew her contract, for which she now was taking legal and employment action. Gill presented herself as the victim of powerful others who conspired against weak and helpless individuals such as herself and that organizations such as universities and professional bodies were just there to support the strong against the weak.

At the beginning of therapy, Gill presented as entirely reasonable and very articulate; at first sight, she was a very credible individual, and she reported that two or three of her junior colleagues had indeed supported her throughout her actions against the male professors and now the university itself. However, the devil was in the detail. As therapy progressed, it became clear that Gill was at the centre of a highly egocentric world in which other people did not, for her, have their own emotions and vulnerabilities – other people existed either to support her or to be against her. Those who were for her, she could in fact work hard to support them, but those whom she perceived to be against her she hated with considerable intensity. Now it turned out that one of the male professors had subsequently retired early with chronic depression following the actions she had instituted against him. Yet she lacked any empathy and experienced absolutely no guilt and no shame for what she had put this person and others through.

In personality disorder terms, Gill showed extremes of narcissism, psychopathy and sadism. Her relationship with her partner was clearly sadomasochistic, and her partner had ended up in hospital on a couple of occasions following their sadomasochistic practices, but again for which she felt no guilt but criticized him for being such a 'wimp'.

There are no effective short-term therapies for severe personality disorders such as Gill's. Whether it is standard cognitive behavioural therapy (CBT), dialectical behaviour therapy, psychoanalysis, or institutionalization, such clients require interventions that last at least a year. In Gill's case we worked together using an emotion-focused approach for over two years; the first step in therapy was helping Gill recognize that she did not have an awareness of other people as separate from her own wishes or control; once she had seen this problem, we then worked on her developing a conscious self-monitoring system for how she was thinking about and evaluating other people's reactions towards her. Gradually, this empathy training began to become a more automatic part of her reactions and feelings towards others and, by the end of therapy, the initial signs of shame and guilt reactions in her began to appear.

Happiness

Living and working in Scotland provides one with the unexpected opportunity to work with individuals from an extreme Protestant Calvinism in which pleasure and happiness are construed as bad and sinful; that is, happiness is a 'negative emotion' in these religious groups, similar to the Ifaluk Islanders in the South Pacific in the famous anthropological study of Catherine Lutz (Lutz, 1988). Some of the Outer Hebridean islands are predominantly Free Presbyterian, which is an extreme form of Calvinism. Now the Outer Hebrides are a long way from the South Pacific, and the bleak beauty of the Islands accompanied by often long and unpredictable Atlantic storms that can blow in at any time of the year add to the melodramatic sense that life is about struggle and suffering and that pleasure would be hard to come by even if not forbidden. The small bleak Free Presbyterian churches highlight the bleakness of this existence; in contrast to the sumptuous indulgences of the Catholic cathedrals, these small bleak churches are completely free of any images, paintings or sculptures; they symbolize the fact that life is a prison from which the only escape is death. Something of the severity of the views can be readily gleaned from the Free Presbyterian Church's website, which declares on its homepage

> Everyone is guilty of sin and deserves to be punished in hell for ever.

My personal favourite on the website is an article entitled 'Why Christians Should Not Celebrate Christmas' which includes the statement:

> The all too common depiction of the Son of God in the form of a plastic doll is therefore nothing short of blasphemous (www.fpchurch.org.uk).

On a holiday to the isles of Lewis and Harris, the extremity of the attitudes was brought home by the owner of the cottage we had rented for a week. She explained to us that we should not play music outside the cottage, not drink alcohol in public, not laugh in public and not to hang washing outside on Sundays. Hanging washing outside on a Sunday was the easy one to give up, because that was not a pleasure any other day of the week either. What we did see on the island, where it was virtually impossible to buy alcohol and there were no pubs, was high rates of alcohol use, which was especially evident on Sunday mornings when there were several cars stuck in the ditches from people driving home drunk late on Saturday night. Alcoholism and depression both occur at much higher rates than in other communities in these islands.

> Andrew had been brought up on the Isle of Lewis but had come to Edinburgh to study medicine as a student. He was now training in psychiatry, but had been off for several months with depression, when his GP referred him for psychological help. Andrew's parents were both strict Free Presbyterians, though Andrew himself presented as more confused about his beliefs. Nevertheless, he still attended a Free Presbyterian church in Edinburgh, and, as I only realized towards the end of therapy, he discussed most of what we spoke about in therapy, with the minister at his local church. Andrew's mother had also suffered from depression, he said for most of her life, but she had refused to ever get any help because it was 'the Lord's wish that she should suffer'. So one of Andrew's major conflicts was whether his training in medicine and psychiatry was also going against the wishes of both his mother and god that people should suffer and die and that we had no right to intervene.

The issue of medicine, psychiatry and the right to intervene seemed to be managed by Andrew realizing the possibility that god could choose to help people through illness and disease by working through other humans and that it was illogical to believe that illness could only be caused by god and cure only by humans. The issue of happiness and pleasure was much more difficult to tackle, especially when I eventually realized that the reason that Andrew would come back at the beginning of each session with arguments against what we had discussed the week before was because his local minister presented him with some feisty rebuttals against him falling for the sins of pleasure and happiness. Although Andrew seemed able to appreciate at an intellectual level that pleasure and happiness were not necessarily sinful, at an emotional level there was never any real change to the rather dour and oppressed feel that Andrew conveyed. Still, some people might say that describes the whole Scottish character, never mind just Andrew. Andrew retained his religious beliefs and had them reinforced on a weekly basis by his minister, and it was clear that the battle of the belief systems was never going to be won by the pleasure-approving hedonists like myself. It was another reminder of the power of religious belief, and how difficult it is to shake such core beliefs. In contrast, Andrew was more open to feeling acceptance of the role of psychiatrist and helper for other people's suffering, especially when he realized that his ministering to the mentally unwell should take account of their belief systems and not just his own.

There are many other less severe examples of where an absence of happiness and pleasure has become the norm in someone's life, not because of core religious beliefs but for more ephemeral reasons. For example, cognitive therapy (Beck et al., 1979) has always emphasized the important distinction between *mastery* and *pleasure* activities, so when clients complete their schedule of weekly activities, they are asked to distinguish between those activities that are done for mastery and those for pleasure. One of the characteristics of depressed individuals is that they sometimes get mastery and pleasure activities extremely out of balance, though often because of very understandable and well-justified reasons.

> Irina had moved to Edinburgh from Eastern Europe seven years before following the break up of her marriage. She had two children now aged 11 and 19 years whom she had brought up single-handedly. Although she was trained in architecture, she had worked long hours initially in the hotel industry to support her family. Subsequently, she did various jobs, including that of beautician, masseuse, events' organiser and tour guide, and for a couple of years, she did all of these jobs at once. While she was working at all of these jobs successfully, she had been able to save enough money to buy a small rundown house but which needed a considerable amount of reconstruction. However, she had been unable to sustain her 'superwoman' approach, as she called it, because about a year before she had begun to experience high blood pressure, which had then led to kidney, oedema and eye problems. She had also been in a tempestuous relationship with a fellow Eastern European who was extremely abusive and unsupportive to her. However, despite her having ended the relationship a few months before she came into therapy, this man would readily harangue her and her children and telephone and call at her house at all times of the day and night.

Irina was in a Catch-22 situation. It had seemed fine when she had been able to work nonstop seven days a week and this had allowed her to provide for her children and pay for her daughter to go to college, to buy a rundown house and begin to refurbish it. Unfortunately, when Irina became physically ill, she was unable to work so much, she had now used all her savings up for her daughter's college, and the renovation and repairs on her house had stopped halfway through and provided a constant reminder to her of her 'failings'. As she became ill, she also felt less interested in her sexual relationship, and her partner began to punish her for not being interested in him instead of supporting her through her illness. It seemed as if the relationship had only provided her with some occasional sexual pleasure, but otherwise he had been a burden on her and now was simply adding to her feelings of stress.

One of the main drivers for Irina was that she had to be super-woman and provide everything while not allowing herself to have any needs or to depend on anyone else. Her unsatisfying relationships to date had confirmed to her that men are unreliable burdens whom should never trust nor rely on. She had fallen in love with her ex-husband as a teenager because he was so handsome, and she had chosen her most recent partner for the same reason. We explored in therapy her negative experiences of handsome men and subsequently whether she could allow herself to be in a relationship with a more caring and intelligent man, rather than one of the fragile narcissist types. She joined a dating agency and after two or three dates and much to her surprise, she started a relationship with a man who was a moderately successful writer and whom she described as teddy bear shaped but who was very caring and intelligent and made her laugh. She said that she had not realized that such men existed and explained that she had previously thought that only women had emotional sensitivity and intelligence because she had never seen such characteristics in a man before. Now before my psychoanalyst-looking-over-my-shoulder says 'What about the transference?!' we explored her narrow view and experience of men in the therapeutic relationship as well as making links to her father and ex-husband. She also said that she thought nice men were likely to be impotent, which is why she had thought she had to go out with a macho abusive type. However, she said that she found her caring writer more sensitive to her sexuality than she had imagined possible, and she began to flourish in her newfound sexual and emotional relationship.

The second area that we explored in therapy was what happens when you ignore your body's warning signals that all is not right. In Irina's case, it seemed to be her circulatory system that acted as an alarm, because there had been an earlier time in her teenage years when she was so stressed that she had had high blood pressure also. So whilst we acknowledged that her high blood pressure could lead to serious physical problems, by helping her to reconstrue her increases in blood pressure as a warning system that she needed to attend to rather than something to get depressed and anxious about, she became less worried about her blood pressure. She also changed some lifestyle habits such as reducing her salt intake and started exercising daily again, which she had stopped because of her concerns about her blood pressure. In the end, we dubbed her new lifestyle as a 'low-salt-high-love diet', a title that she and her new boyfriend are thinking about using for a lifestyle book they plan to co-author. At follow-up, she reported that she and her new partner were now engaged; that he had now moved in with her and had paid for completing the refurbishment of her house. She was still following her low-salt-high-love diet and was thinking about signing up for a master's degree in architecture so she could get back to doing what she most enjoyed. Her blood pressure and general health were now back to normal, and she described herself as the happiest she had ever been. So it seems only right to end a section on 'too little happiness' with a happy ending because, so far, Irina and her 'teddy bear' have been living happily together.

Summary and Conclusions

The purpose of this chapter was to illustrate a sample of the range of problems that can emerge when people experience too little of one or more emotions. As before, we structured the discussion around the five basic emotions of fear, sadness, anger, disgust and happiness. In the case of fear, we considered case examples in which the unacceptability of fear as an experience in men can often be manifested in a range of other problems such as excessive aggression and drug and alcohol problems. However, extreme circumstances such as the loss of a loved one or a life-threatening experience can overwhelm such individuals in that they are unable to cope with the anxiety they then experience.

In the case of sadness, we presented examples similar to those for fear, in which the experience of sadness as an unacceptable emotion can either leave the individual overwhelmed and unable to cope, or as in the case of Dave, completely numbed and unable to experience or do anything following the sudden loss of his partner.

In the case of anger, we raised the possibility that unconscious emotions may be expressed indirectly through dreams, facial expressions and the like and gave the example of Kate who was terrified by repeating dreams of her husband's death, but was never able to experience anger directly with him.

For the emotion of disgust, we looked at possible disgust-based PTSD reactions such as in the case of the emergency worker discovering the decomposed corpse. However, we also considered the complex disgust-based emotions of guilt and shame and suggested that an inability to experience these emotions may be a significant component in some of the personality disorders. One of the implications for therapy that all short-term therapeutic approaches have realized is that interventions with personality disorders are necessarily of a longer nature than those with the *DSM* axis I–type emotional disorders.

The reasons why there may be too little of one or more emotions vary from person to person. Socialization practices clearly play a major part in the determination of acceptable and nonacceptable emotions for boys and girls and vary from family to family, religion to religion and culture to culture. The traditional Western view that fear and sadness are 'weak feminine' emotions and that anger is 'strong masculine' will keep psychotherapists in business for a long time. Thank you, Plato, on behalf of psychotherapists everywhere for being so wrong about emotion (while your student, Aristotle, got it so right!). And thank you, Calvin, Knox and Luther for turning all pleasure into sin. Our cultural and religious traditions seem to have focused on at least one key drive (typically sex) or emotion and turned it into an issue of good versus evil. And we all suffer the consequences of these mistaken religious and cultural views.

Many of the problems seen in personality disorders stem from deficits in the understanding of emotions in self and in others and, given that shame and guilt develop in the second year of life, one would expect that attachment problems, problems in the development of functions that have been variously labelled theory of mind, mentalization or reflective functioning are likely to underlie the problems later seen in the personality disorders (Bateman & Fonagy, 2006). These early problematic strata, which are mostly preverbal and automatized so early in life, are of course difficult and challenging to change; indeed, they may be impossible to change in, for example, the psychopathic- and narcissistic-type disorders where the personality traits are egosyntonic and may provide certain interpersonal advantages.

The final point that we would like to mention is that problems in the experience of and expression of emotions as outlined in this chapter lead to an increased risk in the development of a range of psychosomatic complaints and disorders, including circulatory disorders, cancer, skin problems and gastrointestinal disorders. Part of the reason for this increased risk is that the emotions have characteristic central nervous system and peripheral physiologies that act through many of these systems, as well as having a general impact on immune system functioning. A range of somatization disorders therefore exist in which an emotion-focused psychotherapeutic approach should be beneficial.

7
Additional Topics

In the previous two chapters, we concentrated on the typical range of emotional disorders to which the SPAARS model can be usefully applied. In passing, reference was also made to a range of other disorders beyond the usual emotional disorders to illustrate how emotion can become tied to almost all aspects of functioning and become disruptive or dysfunctional in the process. The purpose of this chapter is not to consider all these additional disorders in exhaustive detail, instead it is to draw attention to these disorders and then to provide a detailed case study of the treatment of a client with bulimia.

In this introductory section therefore, we comment briefly on topics that an emotion-focused approach can provide insights into. In terms of disorders, these include eating disorders, sexual dysfunction, drug and alcohol use, personality disorders and other developmental disorders such as autism.

Eating Disorders

The potential role of emotion in eating disorders has largely gone unnoticed, with just one or two exceptions. The focus has mostly been on the behavioural and cognitive aspects, but we are currently developing models in which the focus is shifted to emotion (Fox & Power, 2009). The following section presents an analysis of bulimia in greater detail, but we also believe that the emotions of disgust and anger play a significant role in anorexia and obesity and that even the focus on 'fear' (as in 'fear of fat' in the definition of anorexia) may have missed the importance of self-disgust (shame) in these disorders.

Sexual Disorders

Relevant work with sexual disorders has tended again to focus on fear or anxiety such as in performance anxiety. However, in relation to sexual disorders again there is a clear role for disgust at various individual and social levels. Kaufman (1989) states:

> In sexual dysfunction syndromes . . . the sexual drive has become fused with shame, either by itself or in combination with disgust and fear (p. 115).

Unlike Kaufman, we would not of course derive shame and disgust separately to each other, but we would concur with his statement that 'fear' has been overemphasized in sexual dysfunction at the expense of disgust and shame, though it is clearly possible that the anticipation of shame could lead to excessive anxiety being experienced in certain situations. For example, as Kaufman argues, so-called performance anxiety is more likely to be based on feelings of shame than it is on fear.

> Early fusion of sexuality with shame . . . is a developmental precursor of adult sexual dysfunction. The patterning of affect with drive is a process spanning years. Sex-shame binds create the nuclei of eventual dysfunction in the sexual life (Kaufman, 1989, p. 146).

Sexual disorders in which disgust may play a major part include vaginismus, dyspareunia and orgasmic dysfunction in women and premature ejaculation, retarded ejaculation and erectile dysfunction in men (see d'Ardenne, 2000, for an overview). A more general impairment of interest in sex, termed 'disorders of sexual desire' by Helen Singer Kaplan (1979), rather than specific impairments may also occur in both men and women. As with many of the disorders discussed in this chapter, the occurrence of childhood sexual abuse often leads to adult sexual dysfunction. Jehu (1988) reported that 94% of a group of women who had been sexually abused in childhood experienced sexual dysfunction in adulthood. However, traumatic experiences in adulthood, for example, following the experience of rape or following childbirth, can also lead to sexual problems in which the individual may react with fear and disgust in subsequent sexual situations. We have also speculated that findings of higher disgust sensitivity in women may not simply be related to food-based issues, but to the fact that women must allow an invasion of their body space by another person's body product (semen) in order for pregnancy to occur; the fact that disgust has a protective role for excluding or expelling 'contaminating' material from the body may provide an important disgust-based reaction in female sexuality (Power & Dalgleish, 2008).

Drug and Alcohol Abuse

The use of drugs and alcohol to alter or amplify mood states is extremely common, and many of the abusers of drugs describe the need to alleviate unpleasant affective states and replace them with more positive affective states. Of course, part of the problem with physiological and psychological dependence is that the withdrawal effects from the particular drug in themselves are affectively aversive, and the user enters a vicious cycle of increased use accompanied by more frequent aversive affect (Powell, 2000). Studies of various addictive states, including in alcohol and drug use, have shown that about 50% of relapse is a result of negative mood states and interpersonal conflict, with a lack of coping or emotion regulation skills being a key part of the problem (Miller et al., 1996). There also seems to be an important role for the associative route in drug and alcohol abuse in that many addicted individuals report cue-elicited cravings that are intense and automatic; for example, heroin addicts report improvements in well-being even as they are preparing to inject so therefore before heroin could have had any effect (Powell, 1995), and O'Brien et al. (1986) found 'highs' amongst opiate users during exposure to cues related to opiate use but without actual intake.

Personality and Developmental Disorders

All personality disorders include emotion dysregulation as core defining features, whether as a result of unpredictable emotion, overwhelming emotion, uncontrolled expression of emotion or lack of appropriate emotion (Livesley, 2000). Problems in socio-emotional development of a more severe nature are also present in disorders such as autism and the autistic spectrum disorders (Hobson, 1995), and Baron-Cohen (2003) has suggested that these disorders may be a more extreme form of the 'male brain' because of their greater prevalence in males. However, we believe that such pseudoevolutionary simplifications ignore the history of Western culture in which reason and emotion have been falsely pitched against each other, with men laying claim to strength and rationality and attributing weakness and emotionality to women. What a mess men make of things when you leave them to do philosophy and psychology! Perhaps now we can start getting it right.

In the remainder of this chapter, we take just one of these possible additional topics, that of eating disorders, to examine in detail the application of an emotion-focused approach and, furthermore, to present a detailed 'realistic' case study to illustrate aspects of the therapy in action.

Bulimia Nervosa

The term 'bulimia nervosa' was introduced by Russell (1979). He argued that bulimia was distinct from anorexia in that many who experienced bulimia neither had associated weight loss nor any history of anorexia. Until then, it had been recognized that many individuals with anorexia showed bulimic-type features, that is, they had times when they binged on food and typically followed by times they purged through vomiting or through the use of laxatives. Moreover, these periods of binging often alternated with periods of food restriction and dieting and other compensatory methods such as overexercising.

Support for Russell's distinction between bulimia and the bulimic variant of anorexia has come from a wide range of other sources and studies (Garfinkel et al., 1980). For example, bulimia is distinct from anorexia on many demographic characteristics; thus, bulimics tend to be older, they are less likely to come from middle-class backgrounds and they are more likely to have a history of antisocial impulsive problems, including shoplifting, drug abuse and self-harm (Mitchell & McCarthy, 2000). As with other eating disorders, the majority of sufferers are women, with the prevalence being about 1% of the population. However, the majority of sufferers remain undetected in the community, with Fairburn and Beglin (1990) and others reporting figures as low as 11% only being known to their general practitioners. Moreover, Fairburn has shown that those that remain undetected and untreated in the community are no less severe than those who are referred for specialist help.

There is also evidence from studies across different age cohorts that bulimia has been increasing in younger generations. In a sample of over 2,000 female participants from a twin register in the US, Kendler et al. (1991) found increasing rates of bulimia between cohorts born before 1950, those born between 1950 and 1959, and those born in 1960 or later. The prevalence for the youngest cohort in this large-scale study had increased to 3.7% in comparison to less than 1% in the cohort born before 1950. Data such as these suggest that the role of social and cultural pressures on dieting and a slim ideal body shape may be leading to this increase in prevalence. A stimulating study of *Playboy* magazine by Garfinkel and Garner (1982) reported that over a period of 20 years the ideal size for female *Playboy* centrefolds had decreased substantially. Studies of dieting in the general population suggest that at any one time approximately two-thirds of women and one-third of men report that they are trying to lose weight, though in actuality there is a continuing increase in obesity in Western populations particularly (Mitchell & McCarthy, 2000). Some studies have also suggested that there may be higher rates of sexual abuse reported by bulimics (Waller, 1992), but the general opinion now seems to be that the rates are no higher than in other psychiatric groups (Freeman, 1998). As Freeman suggests, the elevated rates of sexual abuse in all psychiatric disorders points to abuse as a general risk factor rather than one that is specific to bulimia. Nevertheless, the elevated rates mean that it is essential to assess carefully for abuse in cases of bulimia.

Many approaches to both anorexia and bulimia have emphasized fear-based reactions as part of the aetiology and maintenance of the disorder; thus, Russell (1970) in his classic discussion of anorexia proposed that the anorexic has a 'morbid fear' of becoming fat, a position that he again adopted in his later analysis of bulimia (Russell, 1979). In contrast, we have previously emphasized that the emotion of disgust may play a more important role in both anorexia and bulimia (Power & Dalgleish, 1997); that is, the anorexic may have disgust-based reactions to certain foods that are perceived to be fattening as well as to the body or certain parts of the body which are perceived to be fat. The bulimic when vomiting of course invokes the classic disgust reaction in which nausea and vomiting play a key part, the key action in disgust being the attempt to rid the body (or mind) of an object (or emotion or idea) such as food that is perceived as being potentially harmful to the individual. In the case presented below, I attempt to expand on this feature of bulimia whilst drawing on more general issues in relation to the disorder.

Background to the case

Anna was a 30-year-old recently married woman who had been referred to psychology services because of her bulimia. Although she reported having bulimic symptoms from the age of 22 years, she had never previously been referred nor had she sought help for her problems. The reason for referral at this point was because she was several months pregnant; both she and her GP were concerned that bulimia was associated with an increased risk of foetal abnormalities and that her continued bingeing and vomiting might therefore lead to problems for her child.

Anna's background showed that she was the youngest in her family, with three older siblings, consisting of two sisters and a brother. She described her mother as dominating and selfish, a 'snobbish' woman who thought she had married beneath herself. Her mother had had repeated episodes of depression for much of Anna's life. Anna's father was described as a rather downtrodden individual, but who varied between times of gentleness and times of excessive temper towards his children. He worked as a labourer in a local factory, which he seemed to show embarrassment about, as did Anna when talking somewhat hesitantly about his occupation.

Anna's parents had, not surprisingly, had a chequered history together. There had been several times during her childhood when

Anna's father left home, but he always returned after varying lengths of time. He had gradually developed an alcohol problem and, more recently, had begun to attend meetings of Alcoholics Anonymous (AA). The initial problems in the marriage had led to Anna's maternal grandmother moving in and living with them. Far from being a positive event, this had distressed the children even more, especially Anna as the youngest, because the maternal grandmother was physically abusive towards her. Anna reported that her grandmother was extremely short-tempered and that she seemed to victimize her as if she were the cause of her parents' problems. The grandmother also looked down on the father as not good enough, and Anna remembered her mother and grandmother regularly sitting and bemoaning their lot whilst criticising her father.

Anna described her childhood and adolescence as lonely and cut off from friends and family. She quickly learned that she could not complain about the maternal grandmother's abuse of her because her mother either did not believe her or simply took her grandmother's side. At the same time, the view that they were 'too good' for the small town that they lived in permeated Anna's attitude to friends at school; she was never encouraged to mix with other children, but she also had the feeling that she was different from them in some important ways that made it difficult for her to mix with them. As an adolescent, however, she said that she became something of a 'tomboy', but was also overweight and thought of herself as 'fat' throughout her adolescence. Her next older sister, three years her senior, was always slim and more attractive. The family treated her as special and Anna often felt jealous of her.

Anna responded to the pressures of her adolescence and her family problems by beginning to work hard at school. Her hard work was met with some success and she did well in her exams. She had subsequently gone on to teacher training college and completed her training as a teacher. She now taught mathematics at a local secondary school, with a subsidiary subject in physical education.

Anna had met her husband while they were training as teachers together. They had, after a short courtship, initially moved in and lived together, but they separated because, she stated, he had not been sufficiently interested in her. She then had a short relationship with another man, but had become pregnant almost immediately and had had a termination. This relationship soon disintegrated and she was left very distressed. She turned back to her previous partner, who was very supportive towards her. Not long after renewing their relationship, they became engaged and then got married. She has now been married for seven years, and this was her first pregnancy with her husband. Her husband had not stayed in teaching and had retrained as an accountant. He now ran his own accountancy business and employed two others. She described him as very ambitious and materialistic, whilst being completely work obsessed. He normally worked six or seven days every week and usually until late in the evening. On his occasional Sunday off, he always seemed desperate to play golf; she had given up arguing with him about his golf, because she hated the way he sulked if she stopped him from playing. The relationship was not a confiding one, but much of her emotional life was played out in secret and not discussed with anyone. Even with her one or two female friends, she reported holding back especially on talking about the problems in her marriage. To talk to her friends or to her family about such problems would, she stated, be a 'betrayal' of her husband and her loyalty to him; it would be 'shameful' to talk about her marriage to anyone else.

In terms of her eating pattern, Anna reported that she had become preoccupied with her weight and body shape from about the age of 16. She had then started dietary restriction and had for much of the 14 years since been on one form of diet or another. She had, she stated, initially been 'very successful' in her dieting and had gone from being a 'fat' teenager to one who was extremely slim. In fact, on a couple of occasions she thought she had probably overdone her dieting and had become almost 'too thin'. The first time was when she had gone to teacher training college and the second had been a few years earlier when she had become preoccupied with being thinner to be more attractive to her husband because she thought he was beginning to lose interest in her.

Anna's pattern of bulimia had however started about 10 years earlier. She said that she had first become aware of the possibility of purging by vomiting when she had found her attractive older sister vomiting whilst they were still living at home. Her first re-action had been that the sister was ill with food-poisoning or the like, but her sister had somewhat embarrassedly explained that she used this as a method of controlling her body shape whilst occasion-ally 'overindulging'. Anna had been horrified for some years at the thought of what her sister did, but then reported that she first tried it herself one night at teacher training college. On this occasion she had

had a very serious argument with her boyfriend and felt devastated and alone. She had then consumed what she described as a 'huge quantity' of chocolate cake and felt completely bloated and 'bad'. She then tried vomiting and felt much better, feeling both less bloated and less 'bad'. This combination or coupling of anger and disgust may be an important feature of bulimia (Fox & Harrison, 2008).

Anna's frequency of bingeing and vomiting had gradually increased up to about once per day. For example, during the first trimester of her pregnancy she was bingeing and vomiting at least daily, in part because she had the 'cover' of nausea in pregnancy as an excuse for her vomiting. However, her GP had shown concern at one of her antenatal checks when he thought she was not gaining any weight and was concerned from an ultrasound scan that the baby was small for its dates. She had then 'broken down' and told the GP about her problem and the concern was expressed about the possibility of foetal abnormalities. Since then she had cut down the frequency of bingeing and vomiting to two or three times weekly, which was the rate she had reported at the beginning of therapy, which started towards the end of the second trimester.

Additional assessment

At the start of therapy therefore Anna had reduced her pattern of bingeing and vomiting from approximately daily to about two or three times weekly. Consistent with the focus on body shape and weight that is typical of both anorexia and bulimia (Russell, 1979), for many years, Anna had been preoccupied with maintaining a body weight below what she saw as a critical weight of 9 stone; anything below this weight was satisfactory, but anything above it made her feel miserable. She had now reached this weight in her pregnancy and she found it completely preoccupying. Although she understood 'rationally' that this was a good thing and that it meant that her baby was growing, at an emotional level she felt desperate and wanted to rid herself of excess weight and feelings of misery. She also said that she could feel herself beginning to lose her muscle tone because she found herself exercising less often as her pregnancy progressed; she normally attended aerobics classes, in addition to regular jogging and her work as a physical education teacher. The loss of muscle tone made her feel 'flabby' and 'fat'.

More formal assessment showed that Anna scored as mildly depressed on the Beck Depression Inventory (BDI-II) (Beck et al., 1996), but without anything of particular note. The Robson (1989) Self Concept Questionnaire gave her a score of 81, a value significantly below the normal range (quoted as 132–142). Her scores on the Dysfunctional Attitudes Scale 24-item version (Power et al., 1994) showed elevated scores on the achievement subscale with clear elements of perfectionism.

A dietician's assessment carried out just before the beginning of therapy showed that Anna was eating 57%, of her recommended daily calorie intake, that she had 37% of her recommended iron intake, and 48% of her recommended foliate intake. Dietary supplements including vitamins and minerals had therefore been prescribed, though her continued vomiting meant that it was unclear how often she actually achieved her recommended intake prior to therapy.

Therapy

Initial sessions

The standard cognitive behavioural approach to bulimia includes four key elements: education about the problem, graded behavioural targets, identification of key thoughts and the identification and challenging of the underlying assumptions relevant to the problem (Fairburn, 1997). These features are general characteristics of the cognitive behavioural therapy (CBT) approach (Beck et al., 1979) and provide a useful starting point for an emotion-focused approach to bulimia.

Following the initial assessment and background information gathering, Anna was given a book recommended for information on bulimia, *Bulimia Nervosa and Binge Eating* (Cooper, 1995). The book provides basic information about the disorder and its causes and consequences; it also provides a self-help guide to therapy. Anna seemed particularly responsive to information about the possible damaging consequences of her repeated bingeing and purging. These early sessions not only provide an opportunity to provide information about the client's disorder but also to provide an introduction to the therapeutic model itself. Therefore elements of the model shown in Figure 7.1, which presents an adaptation of the emotion-focused cognitive therapy (EFCT) model for Anna, were presented to her. The basic idea was that the nature of her early relationships both with her

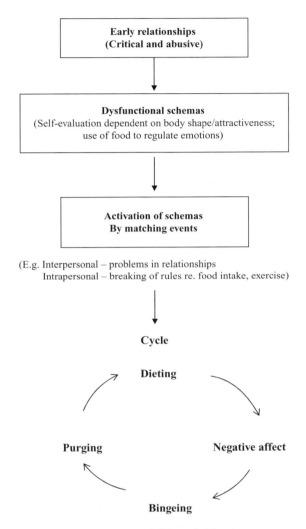

Figure 7.1 An EFCT model for Anna

parents, her grandmother and her older sisters, had on the one hand emphasized the importance of physical shape and attraction but on the other hand left her feeling ugly and unattractive herself. During adolescence, and especially around puberty, she had striven, as many others, to make herself more attractive through continual dieting. However, she had then learned from her sister, whom everyone did judge to be attractive, that dieting in itself might be insufficient. Instead she had been initiated into the secretive world of bulimia, where extreme purging provided even greater control over body shape and size, especially following periods of bingeing. Of course, the initial presentation to Anna did not present the full formulation for her own case, but rather presented the general model while attempting to begin to tie the model into her own particular presentation.

Anna's reaction to the initial presentation and discussion of the EFCT model seemed to be satisfactory. She seemed to recognize herself in some aspects of the model and seemed to begin to apply aspects of the model to herself. In the area of depression, for example, previous research has suggested that the client's reaction to the presentation of the CBT model can provide a good indication of the likely positive or negative response to therapy (Fennell & Teasdale, 1987).

The second stage of EFCT and other CBT interventions for bulimia is to begin to make some achievable behavioural goals to give the client a sense of success and engender hope for more difficult future therapeutic tasks. This task begins with careful monitoring of the daily eating pattern, which includes detail about the food and drink consumed, the situation and whether there was any use of vomiting, laxatives or diuretics (see Fairburn, 1997, for a sample monitoring form). The monitoring forms can begin as straightforwardly as this, but eventually additional columns can be added in order to examine associated cognition, emotion and alternative interpretations, including the more detailed Emotion Diary Form shown in Appendix 5. In Anna's case the first couple of weeks showed a clearly established pattern of no food intake in the morning, occasional 'diet' food at lunchtime but which was still experienced as 'giving in' and 'weak'. She would then eat a 'diet' evening meal, typically soup and salad, which would either be eaten alone or sometimes with her husband. Her episodes of bingeing tended to be concentrated in the late evening either when her husband was still at work, or even if he was at home, he normally worked in his office, and she was able to binge and vomit undisturbed. However, she had also experienced a change in her pattern of bingeing during the second trimester of pregnancy, when she would wake up in the middle of the night feeling ravenous and then report feeling completely out of control and unable to stop herself from bingeing. She seemed to find these late night binges particularly distressing because of the extent to which she felt completely out of control. Her binge food at all times tended to be carbohydrates such as large amounts of bread, biscuits and cakes, which were often present around the kitchen, but which were then carefully replaced the next day to make it look as though they were the original packet or article.

One of the initial behavioural interventions was therefore to attempt to switch Anna's pattern of eating towards a regular three-meals-a-day pattern. Information and feedback were given to her about the consequences of avoiding breakfast and lunch, with effects such as low energy levels, a lowering in mood and increasing the likelihood of bingeing later in the day. Discussions of this issue seemed to make quite a difference, and Anna was soon adding a small breakfast into her daily routine and was no longer avoiding lunch. Within two or three weeks of the start of therapy, the frequency of her binge/vomit episodes had reduced to zero, with the most significant intervention appearing to be the change in her daily eating pattern, making her feel less 'ravenous' in the late evening and during the night.

Subsequent sessions

By this stage, Anna had made changes to her eating pattern and there followed many weeks during which she reported no binge/vomit episodes (see Figure 7.2). During this time she did however cross over from her preferred weight of less than 9 stone into her 'miserable' weight of over 9 stone. She accepted, at least for now, that being pregnant inevitably meant that she would put on some weight, because it showed that her baby was growing healthily inside her. She was also aware of her change in muscle tone, a consequence of being unable to exercise as much. In many ways, the change in muscle tone seemed to make her feel more distressed than her increase in weight per se.

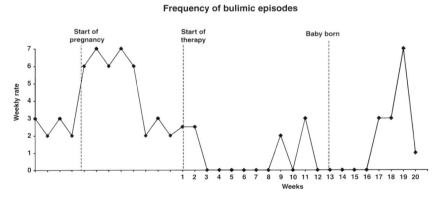

Figure 7.2 A summary of episodes of bingeing for Anna

In order to explore some of the negative emotional states that seemed to be linked with Anna's bulimia, we instituted a structured diary. Although Anna's BDI score was not remarkable, nevertheless, the EFCT formulation clearly linked her emotional reactions and her bulimic episodes. A three-column structured diary was used for the first couple of weeks, with columns representing Situation, Emotions, and Thoughts. She quickly learned to use the three-column diary and found it useful, so she was then switched to a five-column diary that included additional columns for alternative interpretation and outcome. Anna was a very compliant diary taker and continued to value the structured diary homework for the remainder of the therapy.

The main recurrent issue that came up from her initial structured diaries was her avoidance of negative feelings towards her husband. It had been clear from the initial assessment that the marriage had stagnated in many ways for both of them. Anna hoped that having a baby would make her husband more interested in her, or, at minimum, that he would be more interested in the family unit and less preoccupied with his work. If anything, she thought that her pregnancy had made the situation worse rather than better. Since becoming pregnant, he seemed to have been even busier and less available for her both during the week and at weekends. He stated that his reason for being busier was that it was simply a coincidence, that he was experiencing an especially demanding time at work and that his business partner had been unwell.

The classic situation with her husband that upset Anna was one of two types, but with both types leading to the same outcome. The first situation was that they would have dinner together at home, though usually later than she would ideally wish because of him returning home late from work. He would mainly talk about his problems at work or be silent during the meal. Soon after the meal had finished he always seemed 'agitated' until he had gone to work in his study. Anna would not say anything but feel annoyed and hold back her angry feelings. She believed that it was wrong to feel angry towards him because he was working so hard and earning enough to fund a very good lifestyle for her and her children. However, she would then begin to feel more miserable and she would experience urges to binge. Sometimes she managed to resist these urges, for example, through distraction by watching the television or reading a magazine, but at other times she was unable to resist the urge.

The second common situation was also related to her husband. Although she always prepared food for about 8 p.m., sometimes her husband did not return from work at the expected time. Normally he would phone at the last minute and apologize for being too busy to make it home for dinner, but occasionally he would not even phone and she would be left not knowing if or when he would arrive home. She found his not phoning or letting her know to be extremely upsetting; these occasions were almost invariably accompanied by a bingeing and vomiting episode.

In terms of the cycle presented earlier in Figure 7.1, there seemed to be an habitual cycle of getting angry with her husband, not expressing but holding back on her angry feelings, becoming more miserable and 'fed up' as a consequence, bingeing on bread and biscuits in order to change her unpleasant affective state, then vomiting to get rid of these 'fed up' feelings, both in the emotion-related and in the food-related senses of this phrase. This pattern of holding back and not expressing her angry feelings clearly stemmed from the abusive relationship with the grandmother in particular, though she also talked to a lesser extent about her feelings towards her parents. However, she had come to feel completely helpless in the face of her grandmother's aggression towards her and had learned to hide her feelings from an early age; on the rare occasions when she had let go of her feelings, she had been punished even more, and her grandmother had manipulated the mother into taking sides against Anna. So Anna had learned from an early age that angry feelings were dangerous and had gotten her into even more trouble; she learned to hide them and try to rid herself of them in other ways. In adulthood, she now tried to rid herself of these feelings through bingeing and vomiting.

This analysis of Anna's bulimic episodes only provides an account of one of the routes into an episode for her. The analysis does not assume that the only cause of her bulimia was holding back on angry feelings; states such as bulimia come to be multiply determined (Mitchell & McCarthy, 2000) and can serve a wide variety of functions for the individual. In Anna's case, there seemed to be a short-term function that consisted of attempting to rid herself of unpleasant affect such as angry feelings. However, there was also a longer-term function that focused on body shape and size and her perception of her own attractiveness. Somewhere between these two main functions, there were clearly other uses as well, but these two became the main focus of the middle sessions of this short-term EFCT intervention.

One of the main focuses for challenging Anna and for her homework assignments was therefore to begin to express her feelings towards her husband in a 'gently assertive' way. One of her fears about expressing her anger towards anyone was that she might become too abusive, as her grandmother became when she got angry. These fears of being like her grandmother led her to the other extreme so that she avoided almost any confrontation with other people. In fact, one of the useful exercises in therapy was when I was unavoidably delayed and arrived 20 minutes late for the session one day. She seemed a little flustered and on exploration of how she felt about my being late, she became annoyed with me. She expressed her annoyance very appropriately, but soon afterwards became very apologetic and concerned that I might punish her in some way such as through refusing to see her for therapy. She was surprised therefore when I thanked her for expressing her annoyance and gave her feedback on how she was able to express her feelings appropriately and did not come across in an excessively aggressive or abusive manner. This experience seemed to give her heart for trying to confront her husband and express her annoyance with him for his lack of investment in the relationship.

The first opportunity that Anna took to confront her husband was the following Sunday when he announced that he was going to go and play golf for the day. She said that she tried to take the same approach as she had with myself, that is, being aware of her feelings but without losing control or becoming 'too annoyed'. However, after a few exchanges in which her husband initially seemed to be surprised at her attitude, he then became very aggressive and started shouting loudly himself. Shortly afterwards, he stormed out of the house and went to play golf anyway. On relating this episode in therapy she became very upset and began to cry. His reaction seemed to prove that she had been right all along to avoid getting angry with him, because getting angry had only made the situation worse, and they had not spoken to each other since the argument. However, it was interesting to note that she had not had any bulimic episodes during these few days even though she had been very upset.

The fact that the argument had gone so badly indicated of course that not only did Anna have a problem with the expression of anger and other similar feelings but also that her husband had a problem when being on the receiving end of what had seemed like a perfectly reasonable request. A communication analysis of exactly what was said and how it was said did not suggest that Anna had been unskilful in her expression of her anger, but that she had done her best. To understand her husband's reaction therefore, we spent some time exploring his way of relating and his family background. Anna reported that he was very much his mother's favourite and that he was 'spoiled' even as an adult and got away with everything. He was used to having his own way and definitely not used to anyone standing up to him. It seemed that part of what had kept the relationship together from his point of view was that Anna basically allowed him to get away with everything; that she took a very passive and accepting role with him even when she felt otherwise. We discussed Anna's options: She could either 'keep the peace' but increase her own risk for bulimic episodes through 'swallowing her feelings' or help both herself and her husband to begin to explore angry feelings in their relationship and learn how to resolve difficult or unacceptable situations. She somewhat hesitatingly chose the second option, but decided that some practice with more trivial issues than her husband's Sunday golf might be a better place to start and might stand more chance of success.

The following week she reported another attempt to confront her husband. The event had been that her husband had promised to collect some photographs from a shop close to his office. He had returned home in the evening without the photographs and, in fact, had completely forgotten that he had even promised to collect them. Normally Anna would have 'kept the peace' and not said anything, but on this occasion she said she genuinely felt irritated with him and therefore decided to express how she felt. Again, his initial reaction had seemed to be one of shock that she should even think of confronting him, but once this reaction had subsided, he seemed to take on board the fact that she was in the right to feel annoyed as he promised to collect the photographs. Anna was pleasantly surprised therefore that she felt better having confronted him, and that he apologized and even collected the photographs the following day. This small but significant success helped her change her way of relating to him and she gradually began to express her feelings more. Her expression of her feelings did not always meet with success, for example, he never did give up his Sunday golf for her, but even though she did not always change his behaviour, she did at least come to feel better about herself for expressing how she felt.

Anna thereby achieved one of her key goals for therapy – that of expressing her feelings more towards her husband – and this expression clearly helped her bring down the number of bulimic episodes to close to zero during therapy (see Figure 7.2). The second key area to work on in bulimia however, as discussed earlier, is of course beliefs and emotions about body shape and size and their relation to the self-concept and perceptions of attractiveness. This area of focus proved more difficult to work with, though the extent of the resistance was not apparent until later. One of the problems in working with Anna's self-concept and body image issues was that she, at least superficially, seemed to be very compliant with the issues and problems that were raised and discussed in therapy. For example, although we discussed issues about problematic consequences of bulimia, she had not directly experienced negative health consequences for herself, though she did have considerable concern for her child. Similarly, her beliefs about her own attractiveness being linked to a weight of less than 9 stone combined with a certain level of fitness and muscle tone were very entrenched, while again superficially she seemed willing to examine and question such beliefs. For Anna, as for many women with eating disorders, there was a very simple and straightforward equation: less than 9 stone plus feeling fit equalled happy and attractive, over 9 stone and feeling unfit equalled unhappy and unattractive. These feelings were also for Anna only to a small degree dependent on how she actually looked, but were more dependent on somatic sensations of fitness, feelings of tightness or looseness in certain clothes and feelings of physical energy. It seemed that at an intellectual level she was prepared to think about and examine these beliefs, but at a more emotional level these were 'givens' that did not prove to be open to questioning or alteration.

Outcome and follow-up

The end of therapy was brought about by Anna going into labour. We had 12 sessions of therapy by then, with the thirteenth session being cancelled because she had gone to hospital to give birth. By that stage, Anna had experienced only a few bulimic episodes during the 12 weeks (see Figure 7.2), a degree of success that she had never achieved before. The one or two episodes that she reported close to the birth were, she said, owing to the expansion of the baby in the abdominal cavity making even eating normal size meals lead her to feeling bloated because of the shrinkage of the capacity of her stomach. These episodes had not been accompanied by bingeing, but she had vomited because of the problem of feeling bloated.

In other areas of her life Anna reported that her relationship with her husband had improved. She found that she was, at least on some occasions, able to express to him how she felt and that on a proportion of these occasions he responded appropriately, or the issue was resolved in some way. He also became a little more helpful from a practical point of view after the birth of their daughter.

In terms of more formal measures, these were assessed at 11 weeks because her due date was imminent. Her depression score on the BDI had reduced to 14, placing her in the nonclinical range. Her self-esteem score on the Robson Self Concept Questionnaire had increased to 126, which still placed her a little below the normal range (132–142) but significantly better than she had been at the start of therapy.

Anna was next seen for a follow-up meeting about seven weeks after the birth of her child (week 20 on the chart shown in Figure 7.2). She discussed the birth, which she had found a very painful and protracted experience, and reported some weepiness after a few days (the maternity blues), but she had quickly recovered from these and did not currently feel depressed. However, over the past few weeks there had been a very significant increase in the number of bulimic episodes, with the previous week having been especially bad because she had had a binge/vomit episode every day. There seemed to be several reasons for the return of the problem. First, she now reported feeling less concerned about possible physical damage from bulimia because her daughter was now born and seemed to be in perfect health. Because Anna herself had never experienced health problems from her bulimia, she therefore thought again that the warnings about physical damage would not apply to her. Secondly, she had started breast-feeding her daughter because she had read somewhere that breastfeeding helped to contract the abdominal muscles and would help her abdomen return back to its normal shape. However, she was disappointed to find that several weeks after the birth she was still over 9 stone in weight, that her abdomen had not returned to its previous shape and that her muscles still did not feel tight enough. Thirdly, her husband had gone away on business all week. Although her mother had come to stay with her, she found the situation tense and had not felt relaxed while her mother was there.

Finally, Anna stated that she had achieved the primary goal that she had for therapy: She had completed her pregnancy successfully and now had a happy and healthy baby daughter. Whatever else had happened, or whatever other issues had been raised in therapy, now seemed of less relevance and importance. She had developed a lifestyle that included the possibility of bingeing and purging, together with a relatively heavy exercise regimen. This lifestyle helped her to feel thin and attractive, and it now seemed to provide the quickest way back to feeling slim, attractive and fit again. Other women whom she knew from her antenatal classes and who had also had children were already speaking enviously of how she was almost back to her original shape and how they would not have known that she had just had a baby. Such comments made her feel good about herself, and she was determined to regain her shape and size quicker than any of the other mothers whom she knew. She no longer needed therapy therefore, thanked me for my help, and left.

As a footnote to the follow-up, about 18 months after this last session, I received a phone call from Anna stating that she was pregnant again and could I help her 'as before'. At the initial meeting she reported that she had averaged about four or five bulimic episodes per week during the 18 months since we had met. However, because she was now pregnant again, she was concerned about possible damage to the baby and just needed some help to cut down and eliminate, at least during the pregnancy, the bulimic episodes. This intervention was achieved in fewer sessions than previously, spaced out more over the course of the pregnancy. Although we again examined issues about emotion regulation through bulimia, about beliefs about body shape and attractiveness and further issues about her relationship with her husband, it was clear that she would appear to be compliant about these issues in the sessions, but she had no intention of making any long-term changes to her lifestyle. Not long after the birth of her second child, she returned to her pattern of several bulimic episodes per week, combined with a heavy exercise regimen.

Therapeutic failure?

So why should this be defined as a 'therapeutic failure' when the client herself saw it as a therapeutic success, in that she had two healthy happy children, and she had improved her way of relating to her husband? It was clear by the end of therapy that Anna had decided that her main goal had been to protect her child and to reduce any risks that might be consequent on her bulimia. However, once this goal had been achieved and she had completed therapy, she returned to her original pattern with a combination of several bulimic episodes and a heavy exercise regimen every week. When she returned subsequently during her second pregnancy, her therapeutic goal was now explicit; she needed some help to return to a bulimia-free pattern while she was pregnant, but now therapist and client agreed that she would only maintain a bulimia-free pattern while she was pregnant, but planned to return to her bulimic lifestyle postpregnancy. As a therapist, I agreed but with a slightly feigned reluctance to this reduced-aim of therapy, but explained that, nevertheless, I would also wish to review her use of bulimia to maintain her body-shape and to regulate her emotions.

Perhaps in some ways as a therapist I was fortunate to discover, at least eventually, that the client's aim in therapy was very different from my own aim as a therapist. Many therapies proceed without such misalliances becoming so clear. In such cases, clients may either keep the goal of therapy secret, or alternatively, they may themselves be self-deceived because the goal is an unconscious one. As an example of conscious deception, a client may be in therapy to please someone else. For example, I have worked with other bulimic clients who had been caught vomiting by a partner or a member of their family. The partner or family member can often become very distressed and demand that the person with bulimia seeks help; to placate the significant other, the person goes through the motions of seeking help and attending therapy. The misalliance in these cases is that the client is in therapy to placate or reduce the concern of the significant other, whilst the therapist believes that the client is there to change her behaviour. In Anna's case it was her GP who became very concerned and persuaded Anna to do something for the sake of her child.

The second type of misalliance is an unconscious one, which thereby combines both self-deception and other-deception. 'Self-deception' is not necessarily a pathological process, but can arise out of normal processing biases and distortions in everyday processes of memory and perception (Power, 2001). There are many everyday examples of bias, which serve to enhance the role of the self and to protect self-esteem and which should be open to some limited self-reflection. However, under certain circumstances, these normal processes can become pathologically self-deceptive; for example, the early experience of abuse and neglect, and problems in emotional development are two examples whereby atypical developmental pathways can lead to psychopathology in which self- and other-deception is prominent. In Anna's case, there was clearly a developmental problem in her handling of negative interpersonal emotions such as anger. Her abusive grandmother, her inconsistent father, and the failure of both parents to offer her protection and self-belief led to problems in emotional development. Although Anna was nevertheless able to make some progress in dealing with her conscious expression of angry feelings towards her husband, there was still another level of hostility of which she seemed to have no understanding. For example, she was unable to comprehend that her apparent compliance but ultimate rejection of examining and challenging her beliefs about body shape, weight and attractiveness could be experienced as hostile; thus, on trying to feed back the experience of being a therapist where there was such a misalliance, at no time was she able to consider that she might actually be expressing hostility albeit unconsciously. Indeed, in psychoanalytic terms there were clearly transference issues in the therapy, which presumably were linked to her parents and to their failure to protect her but which would have required longer-term therapy in order to begin to address. As we have argued elsewhere (Beach & Power, 1996), such transference issues are not solely the provenance of psychoanalysis but can arise in any form of therapy. However, in Anna's case there was never any possibility of addressing such issues, even during the second spell of therapy, because such issues were outside her therapeutic goals. As a therapist, therefore, I unwittingly ended up with the first 'therapeutic failure', but clearly and explicitly agreed to the second 'therapeutic failure'.

Further comments about Anna

Two additional theoretical comments also need to be made about bulimia, drawing upon the therapeutic work with Anna. The first issue concerns the role of the emotion of disgust in bulimia, a role that has been ignored or minimized not only in the eating disorders, but in many other disorders also (Power & Dalgleish, 1997; 2008). Following in the tradition of Russell (1979) and other key writers on eating disorders, there seems to have been an overemphasis on the 'morbid fear' factor in eating disorders such as anorexia and bulimia. Yet these disorders share such a conceptual overlap with the key elements of disgust reactions; thus, many disgust reactions are related to food and to the by-products of food (including vomit, urine and faeces), whether in relation to their smell, taste, texture or appearance. Everybody has protective disgust reactions to, for example, rotting food and certain categories of food that they may be socialized into not eating (pig products in some cultures, etc.). However, many individuals with eating disorders have their own lists of 'bad' foods, which are typically the foods on which they binge, but are usually defined as 'bad' because of their calorific content rather than their pleasantness/unpleasantness to eat. The purging reaction in disgust of expelling 'contaminated' or 'bad' material from the body then comes to be used in bulimia as the method both of expelling the binged food and of attempting to expel the unwanted emotions, which may on the one hand be the cause of the bingeing in the first place, but which may also be a consequence of the emotional reaction to the bingeing having taken place. In Anna's case there was the clear presence of both functions; she attempted to rid her body of both the 'bad' food that she had binged on and she attempted to rid herself of 'bad' emotions such as anger that could trigger the bingeing, and 'bad' emotions such as guilt and shame that resulted from having given in to bingeing. Disgust is the emotion that eliminates unwanted material from the body; the 'morbid fear' explanation does not account for the combination of bingeing and purging.

A second area of comment arises from the suggestion that Anna experienced anger at both a conscious and an unconscious level and that in spite of being able to work with the conscious level, she had little or no access to her unconscious anger and hostility. Such multilevel views of emotion have clear origins in psychoanalytic theorizing, though interestingly Freud himself thought that *emotion* in itself could only be experienced at a conscious level (see Chapter 1). However, more recent multilevel theories of emotion, of which they are now several influential models, emphasize the need for different levels within good theories of emotion (Teasdale, 1999). As presented in Chapter 1 and 2, within our own SPAARS model, we argue that there are multiple levels of representation, but two key routes through the system to emotion. The first is a high-level route that invariably includes the conscious experience of affect and the second is an automatic or unconscious one that occurs outside the individual's awareness though aspects of it have the potential for awareness. These two routes have different implications for change processes in psychological therapies (Power & Dalgleish, 1999), with the automatic route being the more resistant and more difficult to change, especially in the case of a client like Anna in whom there is little or no acknowledgement of such emotions.

Summary and Conclusions

The purpose of this chapter has been to highlight that an emotion-focused approach has application beyond the traditionally conceived emotional disorders to a wide range of adjoining disorders such as eating disorders, sexual disorders, drug and alcohol abuse, personality disorders and developmental disorders. However, to present each area in sufficient detail would require a substantial tome in itself. Therefore, we have chosen to take one topic, that of eating disorders, in detail and to illustrate the EFCT approach with a case study of a woman with bulimia. A case was chosen that in some ways represented a 'therapeutic failure', even though the client achieved what she had set out to gain from therapy. There is of course a great tradition from Freud's (1905) case 'Dora' onwards in which therapies have gained from understanding aspects of therapeutic failure (see also Foa & Emmelkamp, 1983, for the equivalent in the behaviour therapies). We hope that the current 'therapeutic failure' also conveys a realistic sense of what can and cannot be done in short-term therapeutic work.

8
An Overview of EFCT

The previous chapters in this book highlighted many different aspects of working with emotion in therapy, with a range of different disorders and problems. In this chapter, we attempt to draw together and summarize the key points of emotion-focused cognitive therapy (EFCT) that have been distributed between the different chapters.

One of the key points that we made about the cognitive behavioural therapy (CBT) approach to psychotherapy is that relatively sophisticated models of cognition are now included or have influenced CBT work with different disorders. In stark contrast, beyond the original simplistic idea that cognition causes emotion, CBT and most other therapies work with a lay person's approach to emotion; thus, the man on the Clapham Omnibus will tell you that emotions are things such as depression, anxiety, anger or grief. As therapists, we seem to be happy with the Clapham Omnibus approach to emotion! But having travelled on the Clapham Omnibus many times when I worked in London as a therapist, I did not think any great advances in emotion theory were likely to come from my fellow passengers.

A slightly facetious version of this proposal, which probably works better in a talk than in the written form, is how do we put the 'E' in 'CEBT'? One analogy is that, as we shift from omnibuses to other forms of transport, emotion is the horse that pulls along the cognitive cart. Emotion provides direction and motivation for cognition. Emotion without cognition is a horse without a cart that will run wild and aimlessly. But cognition without emotion is the cart without the horse, which will simply sit going nowhere while endlessly cogitating about the fact that it is going nowhere. So emotion is the driving force for cognition, but the cart and its driver are there to steer the horse in the right direction, to help it stop for food and water when it needs sustenance and to help put its strength to productive use.

The model of emotion that we have based EFCT on is the multilevel approach that Tim Dalgleish and I have developed over the past decade or so (Power & Dalgleish, 1997; 1999; 2008).

In our so-called SPAARS model (in which the letters stand for different types of representation systems – schematic model, propositional, analogical, and associative), we have argued that there are not one, but two routes to the generation of emotion (see Figure 8.1). The 'low-level' route is a direct and automatic one that requires little or no effortful conscious processing and that is there from birth. However, the innate starting points for emotion are forged and altered through developmental and socialization forces that can continue across the lifespan. Around the first to second years of life, the so-called 'self-conscious' emotions such as guilt, shame and pride begin to emerge (Lewis, 2000), which highlight the development of a second 'high-level' route to emotion that is largely conscious and effortful. This conscious and effortful appraisal route continues and develops

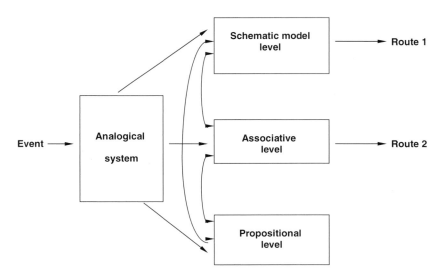

Figure 8.1   The SPAARS model

throughout life, but oft-repeated event-appraisal sequences can also become automated, and the processes and products of the automatic route themselves can become inputs to the effortful appraisal route. So there is a dynamic interaction between the two routes that can be synergistic, can be conflictual, and can enrich our emotional experience much of the time. Various problems can develop from these two routes, including misappraisal, inhibition and rejection of automatic route emotions and coupling of emotions. We return to these problems later in the chapter.

The second key aspect of the SPAARS approach is the proposal drawn from Oatley and Johnson-Laird (1987) that there are five basic emotions: sadness, anger, anxiety, disgust, and happiness. These five provide the innate starting points for socio-emotional development, but a variety of individual, family and cultural forces then shape the range of complex emotions and the expression and display rules for these emotions. As we have argued, families, religions and cultures can have problems with any one of these emotions: Western cultures have traditionally 'genderized' some emotions so anger is seen as a 'strong masculine' emotion and fear and sadness are seen as 'weak feminine' emotions. Religions such as some extreme Calvinist groups particularly in the Outer Hebrides of Scotland construe emotions such as pride and happiness to be sinful and negative – a view that they share with another Island group in the South Pacific, the Ifaluk, so perhaps desert islands are not as paradisiacal as we would like to imagine!

With these points in mind, we now turn to an overview of the practice of EFCT, which is presented in terms of the three phases of therapy that provide a generic framework in which to examine all psychotherapies (Power, 2002): the alliance-assessment phase, the work phase, and the termination phase, which were considered in detail in Chapter 3.

Emotion-Focused Cognitive Therapy

The alliance-assessment phase

Alliance
Therapeutic alliance is the keystone of all psychotherapy, as discussed in detail in Chapter 3. There is a particular pressure in short-term therapies to establish a good working relationship with the client to

gain trust in the therapist sufficiently and share difficult, painful and often shame-inducing experiences. The therapist therefore needs to be highly skilled – on the one hand being supportive and not leading the client into disturbing revelations too quickly (with the danger that the client might drop out of therapy), on the other hand ensuring that a full and complete account is obtained of the client's past and current problems. The skilled therapist must get the balance right between obtaining a full assessment and sensitively exploring difficult issues.

Clients who have no confiding relationships and are highly suspicious of interpersonal relationships provide considerable challenge for the therapeutic alliance and for any work or challenge attempted during therapy. Even when the therapist believes that a good alliance has been established and is therefore actively engaged in the work phase of therapy, 'ruptures' to the alliance can occur suddenly and unexpectedly. In EFCT, there is particular danger with, for example, 'gendered emotions' of causing such ruptures. Examples were provided in earlier chapters of stereotypical Glaswegian male clients for whom fear and sadness were nonallowed emotions, whilst anger was seen overpositively. Working with the shame-related evaluations of fear and sadness in such men led to frequent ruptures in the alliance, in which the work had to stop in order to repair the therapeutic relationship. These repairs involve an exploration of what the client believes the therapist's reactions are towards seeing 'weakness' because he is holding back tears or feeling panic stricken. They are not likely to believe what you say the first time about such 'weak emotions', but as a therapist, you are likely to have to come back time and time again to the issues raised by 'weak emotions' before the client is able to accept them as normal experiences rather than as something to be ashamed of.

Therapy process work has shown that most therapists find their clients' negative feelings towards them especially difficult to cope with, and many therapists may mistakenly avoid such negative feelings being expressed by their clients (Henry et al., 1986). In EFCT it is particularly important that clients first not only feel safe enough to be able to express such negative feelings towards the therapist but also be helped to express such negative emotions in a nondestructive and more constructive manner and not be punished by the therapist. For example, if a client begins shouting and thumping her chair whilst expressing anger towards the therapist, the therapist not only needs to consider both the reason for the anger and whether it is justified but also needs to review the way in which the client expresses her anger. Perhaps as a woman, she may bottle up anger until it bursts into an avalanche that is too destructive. In such a case, the client needs to be helped to express anger not only more often but also more appropriately. And of course the therapist may need to deal realistically with whatever the reason is for the client being angry.

Assessment

An important part of the first phase of therapy is to collect an appropriate range of standardized and other assessment information from the client. Sometimes there are requirements of the service setting in which therapists work for a core set of assessment information, which typically include one or more symptom or distress measures. However, a full assessment for CBT or for EFCT needs to include a many other formal assessment measures, which are likely to provide invaluable information for case formulation and reveal information that sometimes is not obvious only from clinical interview. Everybody and every service is likely to have a preferred set of assessment measures, or perhaps a set that has become 'traditional', irrespective of how useful the measures might or might not be. We have been working on several measures which are specifically designed for assessment for EFCT, but in addition, therapists should of course use whatever other disorder-specific, goal-specific and outcome measures they find useful.

1.　*Emotion-related measures:* The Basic Emotions Scale (BES) (Power, 2006) provides a good starting point for emotion assessment. The scale consists of a set of 20 items derived from the five basic emotions of anger, fear, sadness, disgust and happiness. Each basic emotion is represented by four exemplars, apart from disgust where we are interested in collecting data on disgust (in the form of 'repulsion'). There are three forms of the 20-item scale – the state, trait, and coping versions – in which the respondents rate how frequently they have experienced the emotion in the past week, in general, and how well they cope with the emotion when it occurs. The scale provides an extremely useful clinical assessment to be used at the beginning of therapy. The scale is presented in Appendix 3.

　　The Regulation of Emotions Questionnaire (REQ) (Phillips & Power, 2007) provides an overview of typical emotion regulation strategies used by the client, or what we have called meta-emotional skills (Power & Dalgleish, 2008). Although the scale was initially developed with a sample of adolescents, it is extremely useful for all adult clients as well. The scale groups emotion regulation strategies into internal functional, internal dysfunctional, external functional and external dysfunctional categories. Although the version presented in Appendix 4 asks about emotions 'in general', it is sometimes useful to assess a particular emotion such as anger or panic, if, from the BES, that is likely to be the focus of the therapeutic work.

The Emotion Diary is adapted from the work of Oatley and Duncan (1992) (see Appendix 5). It provides between-session detailed structured information about significant emotion experiences and their context, which can then be explored in therapy and help the therapist choose a problem focus for therapy. The simpler one-page structured diaries that are standard in cognitive therapy should also be used, along with the Weekly Activities' Schedule to get an overview of the client's typical week.

2. *Symptom measures*: There are standard measures for the assessment of symptoms of depression, anxiety, obsessive–compulsive disorder (OCD), posttraumatic stress disorder (PTSD), anger, grief, mania, psychosomatic problems and so on. However, the choice of which measures are used clinically does not always depend on which are necessarily the best measures, but such choices can often depend on 'tradition' and whether or not the measure is free. In Chapter 4 we gave examples of weaknesses in measures of depression that are commonly used, such as the Hospital Anxiety and Depression scale (HADS) and the Beck Depression Inventory (BDI)-II. For example, although widely used, the BDI focuses on cognitive and somatic symptoms of depression but does very badly on emotion (e.g. it does not assess 'shame', which is crucial to assess depression) and the interpersonal (e.g. sensitivity to others, social avoidance). A new measure of depression that we are currently developing and that overcomes these limitations is presented in Appendix 2.

3. *Social support*. One of the strengths of the interpersonal psychotherapy (IPT) approach is its allocation of at least one of the early assessment sessions to what it calls the interpersonal inventory. In this session, the therapist obtains a very full picture of the social network of the individual and the quality of support from the people in the network, in particular, which are the healthy

relationships that can be further developed and which are the difficult relationships that can be better managed. As part of this assessment, we use the Significant Others Scale (SOS) (Power et al., 1988) to assess the level of actual support contrasted with the ideal levels from key significant others in the network (partner, mother, father, best friend, etc.) (see Appendix 6). In working with depressed clients, for example, it is not uncommon to find that the expectations of others are excessively high, which can of course provide part of the therapeutic focus.

4. *Quality of life*: Although measures of quality of life are not yet routinely used in psychotherapy outcome, their widespread use in the assessment of pharmacotherapy outcome means that they are on their way. Because we have been working on developing the WHOQOL measures of quality of life (e.g. Power, 2003), we strongly recommend these measures for use at the beginning and end of therapy, including the WHOQOL-BREF, the WHOQOL-100 and the WHOQOL-OLD, of which the WHOQOL-BREF is presented in more detail in Appendix 7.

5. *Additional measures*: Many other specific measures can be used according to the problem focus chosen for therapy that can assess specific aspects of the therapy intervention. In addition, therapists can think of non-self report measures, such as analysis of audiotapes, observational measures, physiological measures and facial expression coding systems. Realistically, of course, such non-self report measures tend to be used only in research trials, though in many service-based therapies the increasing focus on evidence-based therapies and therapy effectiveness makes the use of non-self report measures more likely. That said, we do believe that all therapists should have formal training in emotion expression coding, especially in the microexpressions that can otherwise be easily missed. Training in facial emotion coding is, we believe, not only useful for the assessment of emotion, but for the ongoing therapeutic work so that the therapist is tuned into this channel of emotion communication, as outlined next.

An emotion facial expression package developed with my colleagues Ursula Hess and Pierre Philippot is summarized in Appendix 1, there is a CD training package that should be worked through, and there are further training tasks provided on the Wiley-Blackwell website (at . . . .). The package begins with straightforward codings of a range of facial emotions, goes on to look at microexpressions of 200 ms embedded in neutral and other emotion faces and then goes on to consider blends of different emotions with morphed emotion faces. We believe that all therapists, whether or not they use EFCT, would benefit in their therapeutic practice from improving their facial expression coding skills.

The work phase

Problem focus

The short-term therapies are at their most effective when they choose a problem focus and thereby avoid the risk of meandering over the disparate and ever-changing problems that some clients present with. CBT's weakness is that there is insufficient guidance in choosing a problem focus and where it gets it right, the choice tends to be driven by the presenting disorder such as panic, or OCD. In contrast, IPT has an explicit framework for problem focus area, which is one of its strengths. For depression in adults these focus areas are grief, transition, dispute or deficit (recently renamed by some as 'interpersonal sensitivity'). However, the IPT focus areas have been developed primarily for the treatment of depression, and it is unclear how these four focus areas might or might not map onto emotional disorders other than depression.

In the case of EFCT, we propose that pooling together the information from the emotion assessment, the clinical background and from the social network should provide enough information for what we call the emotion problem focus for the therapeutic work. In Chapters 5 and 6 we outlined how to work with either too much or too little emotion, but such considerations provide only one aspect of choosing the focus, albeit crucial to know whether each emotion is dysregulated.

The key therefore for the emotion problem focus for the work phase of therapy is to consider the following issues:

- Which emotions are problematic?
- What are the key social contexts in which they are problematic?
- How are they regulated?
- Which socio-emotional focus can be optimally worked with in therapy?
- What are the risks (suicide or self-harm risk, relationship, etc.)?

We have provided many examples in earlier chapters, where the choice of emotion problem focus is not as obvious as it might seem at first sight. For example, in the Glaswegian males referred for anger management, problems often turn out to sadness or anxiety, in which aggression is used as a socially acceptable means of expression and an attempt to rid the sufferer of 'weak feminine emotions'. Similarly, women presenting as anxious and depressed may often have problems in the management of anger rather than anxiety or sadness, but their anger is expressed in the form of anxiety or sadness. Freud was of course misled into thinking that all depression can be explained by such a mechanism, but we are merely suggesting that some depressions in some women might well be formulated as an anger focus and that anger is likely to be contextualized in a relationship problem, for example, with a partner, a parent, a boss at work or something similar. So the problem focus for the therapy could be anger in the partner relationship.

To summarize these suggestions about choosing an emotion problem focus, which is then contextualized into a social relationship or context, the following are examples of what this type of problem focus work should look like:

- Anger – Partner relationship
- Sadness – Bereavement
- Anxiety – Aggression to others
- Panic – Self-overwhelmed.

The emotion problem focus can therefore be elaborated along the lines of those shown in Table 8.1. The first column shows the referring problem, for example, depression. The second column highlights the problematic emotion and the third column the context in which it is problematic, in this case it is anger in the partner relationship that becomes the initial problem focus for therapy. For preliminary formulation and consideration of actual problem focus, there may be several such areas that need to be highlighted and summarized in the case of a particular client. The typical clinical referral may have several such possible problematic focus areas and these may or may not be thematically related to each other; thus, even though the primary focus might be on the client's inability to express anger with her partner, there may be other relationships problems that are thematically related (e.g. anger with parents or anger with boss at work)

Table 8.1   Examples of the emotion problem focus

Referring problem(s)	Problem emotion(s)	Problem context
Marital problem	Anger	Relationship with partner + other significant relationships
Aggression	Panic attacks	Physical and verbal aggression towards others
Depression	Anger Shame	Anger towards others turned against self
Depression	Sadness Shame	Grief over loss of partner
Bulimia	Anger	Negative emotions eliminated by bingeing and purging
PTSD	Disgust Shame	Intrusive thoughts and memories, not shared
Alcohol problems following trauma	Anxiety	Avoidance of public transport following mugging
Bipolar disorder	Elation Anger	Reckless and illegal behaviour when 'high'

but which can be linked back to the focus on anger with partner. In addition, the actual work of helping such a client to learn how to be angry constructively may involve safer relationships or less challenging relationships than that with the partner to begin with. The therapeutic relationship should provide one such safe relationship in which the client can learn how to express difficult emotions such as anger. However, there may be a best friend or sibling or friendly work colleague with whom learning to express anger constructively can also be practiced.

The type of work that is done depends of course on whether there is too much or too little of the emotions that provide the problem focus. In Chapter 5 we considered detailed examples of the experience of too much emotion, such as in cases of grief, panic or depression. Sometimes the emotion regulation strategies that are being used can provide a central part of the formulation for why too much emotion is present. Attempts to inhibit emotions excessively can sometimes, as Daniel Wegner has shown (Wegner, 1994), have the opposite effect and lead to an excess of the emotion. Whereas the capacity to *suppress* an emotion such as feeling angry with your boss and then express the emotion later is a healthy and mature regulation strategy (Vaillant, 2002), the attempts to repress or rid oneself in other ways such as through drink, drugs or aggression can often lead the person to experience more of the emotion rather than less of it. Such a consequence follows from the function of emotions; within SPAARS and other models, emotions typically occur at junctures in goals or plans and the more important the goals or plans the more intense the emotions are likely to be (Power & Dalgleish, 2008). If you want to get married and have children but you find that your partner is having an affair, then the blocking or frustration of goals and plans by a perceived agent (see Table 2.1) will lead to intense anger. However, emotion regulation that only attempts to remove the angry feelings (such as with drugs or alcohol) will do nothing to resolve the situation that is leading to the anger and the avoidance of dealing with this situation may make the anger worse rather than better. In Chapter 5, we considered a wide range of examples from all of the basic emotions of how to work with too much emotion.

In Chapter 6 we considered the problem of *too little* emotion, though as we noted, the person who tries to experience too little of one or more emotions may sometimes experience too much, or, like with the man who murdered his wife, on the rare occasion that the emotion is expressed it is expressed too destructively. When an emotion is socialized out of the child's acceptable range of experience, then the person's self-development is likely to occur with the exclusion of such emotions as egodystonic. An extreme example occurred with the example of Kate in Chapter 6 in which she experienced no angry feelings with her husband or anybody else, but she began to have repeating nightmares in which her husband was killed or injured especially when he went away on business trips. The formulation linked her anger, coupled with her inability to experience or express it, to her husband; the dream material seemed to be the only obvious way in which her hostility was expressed, but we never made any progress in short-term therapy with Kate herself making such a connection. Of course, BT and CBT therapists who have been brought up with a fear of psychoanalysis will dismiss the possibility of 'unconscious emotions' that can be expressed in dreams, in obsessions, in mistakes and in somatic symptoms; perhaps they might have persuaded Kate to enjoy her free time and join the tennis club, where she would now be having an affair with her tennis coach (that will teach her husband a lesson, won't it?). It is possible that such activity scheduling could indirectly help her to manage her unexpressed anger through making her relationship with her husband less important (or even making it nonexistent). But such an indirect method will not have dealt with the source of the problem, and Kate may well seek help in the future when she is unable to deal with the problems with her tennis coach for whom she had left her husband.

In the more extreme cases such as with the personality disorders, the work phase of therapy may need to be extended to a year or more, though where health services are restricted in the number of sessions that they can offer sometimes the therapeutic benefits continue after the end of therapy. The severe personality disorders do in general provide challenges for all types of short-term and long-term therapies, but the important conceptualization of these disorders is that they represent problems in socio-emotional functioning that arise in a developmental context. At the most extreme are the developmental disorders such as autism, which reflect severe deficits in areas such as theory of mind, theory of emotions in self and other and extreme communication problems. Indeed, basic-level training in emotion and emotion skills is often of benefit in such severe developmental disorders. Similarly, in some of the severe personality disorders there may be a need for basic training in emotion recognition and emotion expression; we would recommend that the training package that we have developed for training therapists (see Appendix 1) should also be used where there is any concern about the client's knowledge and experience of emotion.

The termination phase

As we have commented on before, CBT is surprisingly quiet about the issues around therapy termination, especially given that it is a short-term therapy (Power, 2002). In short-term therapies, it is essential to consider the issues about termination right from the start of therapy, because even at the start it is known when therapy will be concluded. In particular, where the presenting problems include grief and depression in which the client has emotional problems because of significant losses, it would seem absolutely essential that therapy termination be explicitly and sensitively dealt with from the start.

There are a number of explicit tasks of therapy termination that need to be dealt with during the termination phase of therapy. These tasks have been most elegantly spelled out in the IPT approach (e.g.

Weissman et al., 2000), and we would recommend that therapists from all therapy approaches are aware of and adapt the IPT approach for use within their own practice. The following points will therefore draw heavily on the knowledge and experiences of IPT therapists. In their excellent clinician's guide to IPT, Stuart and Robertson (2003) highlight the following issues in relation to termination of treatment for depression:

- Facilitation of the client's independent functioning
- Enhancement of the client's sense of competence
- Reinforcement of new communication behaviour
- Reinforcement of the use of social support
- Positive reinforcement of the client's gains
- Acknowledgement of client's sense of loss
- Exploration of client's feelings about therapy termination
- Therapist self-disclosure of feelings about conclusion
- Mutual feedback about therapy and review
- Management of any posttherapy contacts

Additional issues to these that have more recently been considered in CBT approaches include *relapse prevention* work, which also seems crucial in dealing with over the final sessions. In EFCT, the problem focus area needs to be reviewed so that when the same or similar stressors occur in the future, the client talks through in therapy how he or she is likely to deal differently with the problems that first brought them into therapy. The risk of course is that under the same psychosocial stressors in the future, the client will lapse back into the old habitual tried-and-tested methods of emotion regulation that contributed to the problems in the past.

We also recommend that at the end of therapy, there should be a formal assessment that repeats some of the measures that were used at the beginning of therapy and the results of which should be fed back to the client in the last session or two of therapy. These end of therapy measures do not need to be as extensive as the initial assessment measures, but should include the most appropriate symptom measure, the BES, the REQ and a measure of quality of life such as the WHOQOL-BREF (see Appendices for these measures). It is tangible feedback for both therapist and client to review these measures in comparison to beginning of therapy values and then to deal with both the positive gains and any remaining areas of concern openly and realistically.

Miscellaneous Issues

All therapies need to develop an evidence-base that is relevant to their practice. In relation to outcome studies, there are many levels of such evidence that are typically accumulated in the order single case studies, non-randomized trials, and then randomized clinical trials (RCTs). Even for standard CBT, there are relatively few RCTS that are based on clinically diagnosed populations, which compare different types of psychotherapy, in which there are at least two appropriately trained therapists per therapy condition and in which adherence to therapy is assessed from audio or video session recordings (see Freeman & Power, 2007). Although there is much political use of the notion of evidence-based therapies, the high-quality evidence meeting the criteria just listed is extremely meagre. We therefore consider it essential for a continuing effort to collect such evidence about all therapies.

However, from the practising therapist's viewpoint, such clinical outcome data may be of less interest than process research, especially when this can also be used to improve personal therapeutic practice. The use of audiotapes with some clients also provides the best form of information for supervision, whether this takes the form of formal or informal therapy training, or peer supervision. Tapes also permit the therapist to revisit problematic or confusing sections of therapy, in which the opportunity to review difficult sections of therapy can also improve therapeutic practice.

Personal therapy also provides an interesting area of debate for different schools of therapy. The views on personal therapy range from it being obligatory for training in psychodynamic therapies to almost an antipathy for many BT and CBT therapists. The problem is that most short-term therapy practitioners would not find their own short-term therapies of personal use, because the therapies have a symptom or specific problem focus. The types of issues that therapists are likely to find beneficial to explore in therapy tend to be more fundamental existential and interpersonal issues and which are more likely to be dealt with in the longer-term psychodynamic therapies.

But if a CBT therapist opposes psychodynamic therapies on whatever grounds, he or she will miss the opportunity to get a feel for therapy from the clients' perspective; rather akin to teaching parenting skills without ever having had your own children, which, although, possible, may be less convincing without personal experience of the role. Our personal recommendation therefore is that all therapists should have their own personal therapy both in order to explore their own motivations for wishing to become therapists and in order to experience therapy from the client's perspective.

Summary and Conclusions

In this final chapter, we have attempted to provide a brief overview of the practice of EFCT without going into the clinical and other details presented in earlier chapters. We hope that we have gone some way to persuade you, the reader, that a focus on emotion has long been absent from the practice of the CBT therapies, that despite a focus on affect in both IPT and psychodynamic therapies, there is either no theory of 'affect' (in IPT) or that the psychoanalytic account of emotion is wrong (Power & Dalgleish, 2008). Academic emotion theory has made significant advances since the 1960s and has finally followed the trail of important clues placed there by Aristotle, Descartes and Darwin. However, until now there has been no emotion-focused approach to therapy that has taken as its base modern advances in emotion research. We believe that the SPAARS approach provides a firm foundation on which to build therapeutic practice that focuses on our troubles with emotion, for our long and difficult misconstruals of emotion have seen us pitch reason against emotion, seeing certain emotions excluded from men or women's experiences because they are too strong or too weak, too feminine or too masculine. In contrast, we believe that every one of us has five basic emotions which guide our development, our interactions and our understanding of the world right from the start of life. What we do with these developmental guides can either lead us towards fulfilling and productive lives or into states of misery and conflict. A therapy therefore that can explore and examine some of that misery and conflict is, we hope, a first step towards a healthier and more appropriate view of our emotional selves.

Appendices

Appendix 1: Emotion Training Package

The emotion training package is attached in the form of a CD and is also available on the Wiley website at ....

Appendix 2: Depression Scale

The New Multi-dimensional Depression Scale (version 2)

Name:_____ Age:_____ Sex:_____
Main Presenting Problem:_____

Instructions: This questionnaire contains 48 items about how you have been feeling recently. Please read each item carefully and circle the number on the scale which best describes your feelings **during the past two weeks, including today** from 1 = not at all to 5 = all of the time.

Items					
How much have you felt:	**Not at all**	**Seldom**	**Quite often**	**Very often**	**All of the time**
1. Low mood	1	2	3	4	5
2. Sadness	1	2	3	4	5
3. Low spirits	1	2	3	4	5
4. Gloominess	1	2	3	4	5
5. Sad mood	1	2	3	4	5
6. Guilt	1	2	3	4	5
7. Unhappiness	1	2	3	4	5
8. Not cheerful	1	2	3	4	5
9. Irritable mood	1	2	3	4	5
10. Bad mood	1	2	3	4	5
11. Shame	1	2	3	4	5
12. Anxiety	1	2	3	4	5
13. Feelings of hopelessness	1	2	3	4	5
14. Loss of interest	1	2	3	4	5
15. No pleasure	1	2	3	4	5
16. The future feels bleak	1	2	3	4	5
17. Feeling worthless	1	2	3	4	5
18. Poor concentration	1	2	3	4	5
19. Self-blame	1	2	3	4	5
20. Life feels meaningless	1	2	3	4	5
21. Feeling a failure	1	2	3	4	5
22. Ruminations	1	2	3	4	5
23. Thoughts of suicide	1	2	3	4	5
24. Unable to make decisions	1	2	3	4	5
25. Low energy	1	2	3	4	5
26. Problems with sleeping	1	2	3	4	5
27. Change in appetite	1	2	3	4	5
28. Lower sex drive	1	2	3	4	5
29. Feeling slowed down	1	2	3	4	5
30. Fatigue	1	2	3	4	5
31. Change in weight	1	2	3	4	5
32. Crying	1	2	3	4	5
33. Agitation	1	2	3	4	5
34. Slowed movement	1	2	3	4	5
35. More pain sensitivity	1	2	3	4	5
36. Intestinal problems	1	2	3	4	5
37. Decrease in activities	1	2	3	4	5

Items					
How much have you felt:	**Not at all**	**Seldom**	**Quite often**	**Very often**	**All of the time**
38. Social withdrawal	1	2	3	4	5
39. Feeling worse than others	1	2	3	4	5
40. Feel a burden on others	1	2	3	4	5
41. Social avoidance	1	2	3	4	5
42. Feeling undeserving of others care	1	2	3	4	5
43. Over-sensitive to criticism	1	2	3	4	5
44. Feeling less attractive than others	1	2	3	4	5
45. Feeling too sensitive to others	1	2	3	4	5
46. Feeling let down by others	1	2	3	4	5
47. Unable to love others	1	2	3	4	5
48. Aggression towards others	1	2	3	4	5
49. Poor memory	1	2	3	4	5
50. Unable to plan things	1	2	3	4	5
51. Feeling disorganised	1	2	3	4	5
52. Unable to care for myself	1	2	3	4	5

Items 1–12 are added together to give a total for the Emotion subscale.
Items 13–24 are added together to give a total for the Cognitive subscale.
Items 25–36 are added together to give a total for the Somatic subscale.
Items 37–48 are added together to give a total for the Interpersonal subscale.
Items 49–52 are possible additional items for the Cognitive subscale.

See Power and Cheung (in preparation) for further details.

Appendix 3: Basic Emotions Scale

The Basic Emotions Scale (General)

The purpose of this scale is to find out about how much or how often you experience certain emotions and then to ask some questions about how you feel actually during particular emotions themselves.

The first part of the scale is designed to explore how you feel **in general**. For each emotion, please circle **one** number only between 1 and 7, to indicate **how often** you feel the emotion.

Remember, for each question please circle **one** number only between 1 and 7 to indicate how you feel.

In general, I feel this emotion:

	Never		Sometimes			Very often	
Anger	1	2	3	4	5	6	7
Despair	1	2	3	4	5	6	7
Shame	1	2	3	4	5	6	7
Anxiety	1	2	3	4	5	6	7
Happiness	1	2	3	4	5	6	7
Frustration	1	2	3	4	5	6	7
Misery	1	2	3	4	5	6	7
Guilt	1	2	3	4	5	6	7
Nervousness	1	2	3	4	5	6	7
Joy	1	2	3	4	5	6	7
Irritation	1	2	3	4	5	6	7
Gloominess	1	2	3	4	5	6	7
Humiliated	1	2	3	4	5	6	7
Tense	1	2	3	4	5	6	7
Loving	1	2	3	4	5	6	7
Aggression	1	2	3	4	5	6	7
Mournful	1	2	3	4	5	6	7
Blameworthy	1	2	3	4	5	6	7
Worried	1	2	3	4	5	6	7
Cheerful	1	2	3	4	5	6	7

Items 1, 6, 11 and 16 add together to give the Anger subscale.
Items 2, 7, 12 and 17 add together to give the Sadness subscale.
Items 3, 8, 13 and 18 add together to give the Disgust subscale.
Items 4, 9, 14 and 19 add together to give the Anxiety subscale.
Items 5, 10, 15 and 20 add together to give the Happiness subscale.

See Power (2006) for further information.

Appendix 4: Regulation of Emotions Questionnaire

Regulation of Emotions Questionnaire 2

We all experience lots of different feelings or emotions. For example, different things in our lives make us feel happy, sad, angry and so on.

The following questions ask you to think about **how often** you do certain things **in response to your emotions**. You do not have to think about specific emotions but just how often you **generally** do the things listed below.

Please tick the box corresponding to the answer that fits best. We all respond to our emotions in different ways so there are no right or wrong answers.

In GENERAL **how do you respond to your emotions?**	Never	Seldom	Often	Very Often	Always
1. I talk to someone about how I feel	O	O	O	O	O
2. I take my feelings out on others verbally (e.g. shouting, arguing)	O	O	O	O	O
3. I seek physical contact from friends or family (e.g. a hug, hold hands)	O	O	O	O	O
4. I review (rethink) my thoughts or beliefs	O	O	O	O	O
5. I harm or punish myself in some way	O	O	O	O	O
6. I do something energetic (e.g. play sport, go for a walk)	O	O	O	O	O
7. I dwell on my thoughts and feelings (e.g. It goes round and round in my head and I can't stop it)	O	O	O	O	O

In GENERAL **how do you respond to your emotions?**	Never	Seldom	Often	Very Often	Always
8. I ask others for advice	O	O	O	O	O
9. I review (rethink) my goals or plans	O	O	O	O	O
10. I take my feelings out on others physically (e.g. fighting, lashing out)	O	O	O	O	O
11. I put the situation into perspective	O	O	O	O	O
12. I concentrate on a pleasant activity	O	O	O	O	O
13. I try to make others feel bad (e.g. being rude, ignoring them)	O	O	O	O	O
14. I think about people better off and make myself feel worse	O	O	O	O	O
15. I keep the feeling locked up inside	O	O	O	O	O
16. I plan what I could do better next time	O	O	O	O	O
17. I bully other people (e.g. saying nasty things to them, hitting them)	O	O	O	O	O
18. I take my feelings out on objects around me (e.g. deliberately causing damage to my house, school or outdoor things)	O	O	O	O	O
19. Things feel unreal (e.g. I feel strange, things around me feel strange, I daydream)	O	O	O	O	O
20. I telephone friends or family	O	O	O	O	O
21. I go out and do something nice (e.g. cinema, shopping, go for a meal, meet people)	O	O	O	O	O

The Revised REQ 21-Item Measure: Scales, Items & Strategies

1) Internal-Dysfunctional:	-'I harm or punish myself in some way' (*self-harm*)
	-'I dwell on my thoughts and feelings (e.g. it goes round and round in my head and I can't stop it)' (*rumination*)
	-'I think about people better off than myself and make myself feel worse' (*negative social comparison*)
	-'I keep the feeling locked up inside' (*repression*)
	-'Things feel unreal (e.g. I feel strange, things around me feel strange, I daydream)' (*de-realisation*)
2) Internal-Functional:	-'I review (re-think) my thoughts or beliefs' (*positive re-apprasial*)
	-'I review (re-think) my goals or plans' (*modification of goals*)
	-'I plan what I could do better next time' (*planning*)
	-'I put the situation into perspective' (*perspective*)
	-'I concentrate on a pleasant activity' (*concentration*)
3) External-Dysfunctional:	-'I bully other people (e.g. saying nasty things to them, hitting them)' (*bullying*)
	-'I take my feelings out on other people verbally (e.g. shouting, arguing)' (*verbal assault*)
	-'I take my feelings out on other people physically (e.g. fighting, lashing out)' (*physical assault*)
	-'I try to make others feel bad (e.g. being rude, ignoring them)' (*making others feel bad*)
	-'I take my feelings out on objects around me (e.g. deliberately causing damage to my house, school or outdoor things)' (*lashing out at objects*)
4) External-Functional:	-'I talk to someone about how I feel' (*expression of feelings*)
	-'I ask others for advice' (*advice seeking*)
	-'I seek physical contact from friends or family (e.g. a hug, hold hands)' (*physical contact*))
	-'I do something energetic (e.g. play sport, go for a walk)' (*exercise*)
	- I telephone friends or family (*new item 1*)
	- I go out and do something nice (e.g. cinema, shopping, go for a meal, meet people) (*new item 2*)

The items are each scored on a scale of 1– 5 and then the mean score is calculated for each of the subscales.

See Phillips and Power (2007) for further details.

Appendix 5: Emotion Diary

Emotion Diary

Cover page

We would like you to keep this special diary of your emotions and moods in the next few days.

You can recognise an emotion when

- **a bodily sensation happens** (such as your heart beating faster), **or**
- **you have thoughts coming into your mind that are hard to stop, or**
- **you find yourself acting or feeling like acting emotionally**

You can recognise a mood when

- you have a feeling of some kind that lasts for more than about an hour

Please complete a diary page as soon as possible after any emotion or mood happens that is strong enough for you to notice.

Please do one page for each of your **next two emotions or moods**. They may be different or the same kind.

DIARY PAGE

Fill a diary page (both sides) when you have an emotion or mood.

1. Was it an emotion ☐ or mood ☐ ? (Please tick one)

2. What is your name for that emotion or mood?..

3. Would you call it a type of any of the following ? (Tick one)
    Happiness/joy   ☐
    Sadness/grief   ☐
    Anger/irritation   ☐
    Fear/anxiety   ☐
    Disgust/shame   ☐

4. How sure are you about your choice in question 3? (Ring one below)
    Not sure at all 0 1 2 3 4 5 6 7 8 9 10 Completely sure

5. How strong was the feeling? (Ring one below)
    Not really noticeable 0 1 2 3 4 5 6 7 8 9 10 As intense as I
                                                               have ever felt

6. Did you have any bodily sensations? (Tick one or more)
    Tenseness (of body, jaw, fists)   ☐
    Trembling   ☐
    Stomach (nausea, churning, butterflies)   ☐
    Heart beating noticeably   ☐
    Feeling sweaty   ☐
    Feeling hot   ☐
    Feeling cold   ☐

    Other ☐ (Please state)..

7. Did <u>thoughts come into your mind that were hard to stop</u> and make it hard
    to concentrate on anything else? (Tick one or more)

    Replaying an incident from the past   ☐
    Thinking about how something might happen in the future ☐
    Longing for someone, or something   ☐
    Thinking about how to get even or get your own back   ☐
    Other thoughts   ☐

8. Did you <u>act or feel like acting in some way</u> ? (Tick one or more)
    Did you generally act emotionally, such as talking a lot, or not at all ? ☐
    Did you make a facial expression, such as laughing, crying, frowning ? ☐
    Did you feel an urge to act or actually act emotionally towards someone, by
        moving closer or touching   ☐
        making an aggressive move   ☐
        withdrawing   ☐
        other   ☐

9. When did the emotion or mood start? Time........................ Date........................

    Roughly how long did it last?........................hours ....minutes

10.   What kind of thing caused the emotion or mood? (Tick one)
      Somebody said something, did something, or didn't do something   ☐
      Something you did, or didn't do   ☐
      You remembered a past experience   ☐
      You imagined something that could happen   ☐
      Something you read, heard about, or saw on tv, film, theatre   ☐
      It seemed not to be caused by anything in particular   ☐
      None of the above ☐(Please state)..

11.   Were you with anyone? (Tick one or more)
      Alone ☐Husband/Wife/Lover ☐ Family   ☐Friend or Friends ☐
      Acquaintances or strangers ☐

12.   Please say briefly in your own words what you were doing, and what happened, if
      anything, to start the emotion or mood:
      ....
      ....
      ....
      ....
      ....

13.   Was the feeling mixed, so that there was more than one emotion or mood at
      exactlythe same time? (Tick one) No ☐   Not sure ☐   Yes   ☐
      If Yes , what emotions or moods were in the mixture?
      ....   and..   .....

14.   Did the emotion or mood stay the same or did it change? For instance, did you start
      feeling angry and later feel sad, or feel happy and later anxious, or suchlike?
      (Tick one)
      It was the same until it finished ☐   It changed   ☐
      If it changed: Please say from what...............................to what..................................

15.   Did the emotion or mood make it harder or easier for you to do something you
      were going to do?   (Tick one)
      Made things more difficult ☐   Made no difference   ☐   Made things easier   ☐

16.   Did you wish at any stage that y ou were not experiencing the emotion?
      Yes   ☐   No   ☐
      Did you try to hide the emotion from anyone else?
      Yes   ☐   No   ☐
      Did you try to stop the emotion from occurring?
      Yes   ☐   No   ☐

17.   About how long after the emotion or mood are you filling in this page?
      ....hours   ....minutes

Source : Adapted from Oatley and Duncan (1992).

Appendix 6: The Significant Others Scale

The Significant Others Scale (SOS) (Power, Champion and Aris, 1988).

Listed below are various sources of personal and social support on which you may be able to draw. For each source of support please circle a number from 1 to 7 to show how well support is provided. The second part of each question asks you to rate how you would like things to be if they were exactly as you hoped for. As before, please put a circle around one number between 1 to 7 to show what your rating is.

Please note: If a particular source of support does not exist for you, please leave the section blank.

Section 1 - Your Partner

		Never		Sometimes		Always		
1	a) Can you trust, talk to frankly and share your feelings with your partner?	1	2	3	4	5	6	7
	b) What rating would your ideal be?	1	2	3	4	5	6	7
2	a) Can you lean on and turn to your partner in times of difficulty?	1	2	3	4	5	6	7
	b) What rating would your ideal be?	1	2	3	4	5	6	7
3	a) Does he or she give you practical help?	1	2	3	4	5	6	7
	b) What would your ideal be?	1	2	3	4	5	6	7
4	a) Can you spend time with him or her socially?	1	2	3	4	5	6	7
	b) What rating would your ideal be?	1	2	3	4	5	6	7

Section 2 - Mother

		Never		Sometimes		Always		
1	a) Can you trust, talk to frankly and share your feelings with your mother?							
	b) What rating would your ideal be?	1	2	3	4	5	6	7
		1	2	3	4	5	6	7
2	a) Can you lean on and turn to your mother in times of difficulty?							
	b) What rating would your ideal be?	1	2	3	4	5	6	7
		1	2	3	4	5	6	7
3	a) Does she give you practical help?							
	b) What rating would your ideal be?	1	2	3	4	5	6	7
		1	2	3	4	5	6	7
4	a) Can you spend time with her socially?							
	b) What rating would your ideal be?	1	2	3	4	5	6	7
		1	2	3	4	5	6	7

Section 3 - Best Friend

		Never		Sometimes		Always		
1	a) Can you trust, talk to frankly and share your feelings with your best friend?							
	b) What rating would your ideal be?	1	2	3	4	5	6	7
		1	2	3	4	5	6	7
2	a) Can you lean on and turn to your best friend in times of difficulty?							
	b) What rating would your ideal be?	1	2	3	4	5	6	7
		1	2	3	4	5	6	7
3	a) Do they give you practical help?							
	b) What rating would your ideal be?	1	2	3	4	5	6	7
		1	2	3	4	5	6	7
4	a) Can you spend time with them socially?							
	b) What rating would your ideal be?	1	2	3	4	5	6	7
		1	2	3	4	5	6	7

Source: Power et al., 1988.

The example shown is for three role-relationships, but the scale is normally designed to assess up to 7 lifestage appropriate relationships (e.g. the above example could be expanded to include father, brother, sister, son, daughter, etc.)

Appendix 7: The WHOQOL Measures

WHOQOL-BREF (see Power, 2003, for further information and information about other WHOQOL measures)

Instructions

This assessment asks how you feel about your quality of life, health, or other areas of your life. **Please answer all the questions**. If you are unsure about which response to give to a question, **please choose the one** that appears most appropriate. This can often be your first response.

Please keep in mind your standards, hopes, pleasures and concerns. We ask that you think about your life **in the last two weeks**. For example, thinking about the last two weeks, a question might ask:

		Not at all	*Not much*	*Moderately*	*A great deal*	*Completely*
	Do you get the kind of support from others that you need?	1	2	3	4	5

You should circle the number that best fits how much support you got from others over the last two weeks. So you would circle the number 4 if you got a great deal of support from others as follows.

		Not at all	*Not much*	*Moderately*	*A great deal*	*Completely*
	Do you get the kind of support from others that you need?	1	2	3	4	5

You would circle number 1 if you did not get any of the support that you needed from others in the last two weeks. Please read each question, assess your feelings, and circle the number on the scale for each question that gives the best answer for you.

		Very poor	Poor	Neither poor nor good	Good	Very good
1	How would you rate your quality of life?	1	2	3	4	5

		Very dissatisfied	Dissatisfied	Neither satisfied nor dissatisfied	Satisfied	Very satisfied
2	How satisfied are you with your health?	1	2	3	4	5

The following questions ask about **how much** you have experienced certain things in the last two weeks.

		Not at all	A little	A moderate amount	Very much	An extreme amount
3	To what extent do you feel that (physical) pain prevents you from doing what you need to do?	1	2	3	4	5
4	How much do you need any medical treatment to function in your daily life?	1	2	3	4	5
5	How much do you enjoy life?	1	2	3	4	5
6	To what extent do you feel your life to be meaningful?	1	2	3	4	5

		Not at all	*A little*	*A moderate amount*	*Very much*	*Extremely*
7	How well are you able to concentrate?	1	2	3	4	5
8	How safe do you feel in your daily life?	1	2	3	4	5
9	How healthy is your physical environment?	1	2	3	4	5

The following questions ask about **how completely** you experience or were able to do certain things in the last two weeks.

		Not at all	*A little*	*Moderately*	*Mostly*	*Completely*
10	Do you have enough energy for everyday life?	1	2	3	4	5
11	Are you able to accept your bodily appearance?	1	2	3	4	5
12	Have you enough money to meet your needs?	1	2	3	4	5
13	How available to you is the information that you need in your day-to-day life?	1	2	3	4	5
14	To what extent do you have the opportunity for leisure activities?	1	2	3	4	5

		Very poor	*Poor*	*Neither poor nor good*	*Good*	*Very good*
15	How well are you able to get around?	1	2	3	4	5

The following questions ask you to say how **good or satisfied** you have felt about various aspects of your life over the last two weeks.

		Very dissatisfied	Dissatisfied	Neither satisfied nor dissatisfied	Satisfied	Very satisfied
16	How satisfied are you with your sleep?	1	2	3	4	5
17	How satisfied are you with your ability to perform your daily living activities?	1	2	3	4	5
18	How satisfied are you with your capacity for work?	1	2	3	4	5
19	How satisfied are you with yourself?	1	2	3	4	5
20	How satisfied are you with your personal relationships?	1	2	3	4	5
21	How satisfied are you with your sex life?	1	2	3	4	5
22	How satisfied are you with the support you get from your friends?	1	2	3	4	5
23	How satisfied are you with the conditions of your living place?	1	2	3	4	5
24	How satisfied are you with your access to health services?	1	2	3	4	5
25	How satisfied are you with your transport?	1	2	3	4	5

The following question refers to **how often** you have felt or experienced certain things in the last two weeks.

		Never	Seldom	Quite often	Very often	Always
26	How often do you have negative feelings such as blue mood, despair, anxiety, depression?	1	2	3	4	5

References

Allan, K. & Burridge, K. (2006). *Forbidden Words: Taboo and the Censoring of Language*. Cambridge: Cambridge University Press.

Andrews, B. (1995). Bodily shame as a mediator between abusive experiences and depression. *Journal of Abnormal Psychology*, **104**, 277–285.

American Psychiatric Association (1994). *Diagnostic and Statistical Manual of Mental Disorders* (4th edn.). Washington, D.C.: American Psychiatric Association.

Aristotle (1947). Nicomachean ethics [W.D. Ross, trans.]. In R. McKeon (ed.), *Introduction to Aristotle*, pp. 300–543. New York: Modern Library.

Bar-On, R. (1997). *The Bar-On Emotional Quotient Inventory (EQ-i): A Test of Emotional Intelligence*. Toronto: Multi-Health Systems.

Baron-Cohen, S. (2004). *The Essential Difference*. London: Penguin Books.

Barrett, K.C., Zahn-Waxler, C. & Cole, P.M. (1993). Avoiders versus amenders: Implications for the investigation of guilt and shame during toddlerhood? *Cognition and Emotion*, **7**, 481–505.

Bateman, A. & Fonagy, P. (2006). *Mentalization-based Treatment for Borderline Personality Disorder: A Practical Guide*. Oxford: Oxford University Press.

Beach, K. & Power, M.J. (1996). Transference: An empirical investigation across a range of cognitive-behavioural and psychoanalytic therapies. *Clinical Psychology and Psychotherapy*, **3**, 1–14.

Bebbington, P. (2004). The classification and epidemiology of unipolar depression. In M.J. Power (ed.), *Mood Disorders: A Handbook of Science and Practice*. Chichester: Wiley.

Beck, A.T. (1976). *Cognitive Therapy and the Emotional Disorders*. New York: Meridian.

Beck, A.T. (1996). Beyond belief: A theory of modes, personality, and psychopathology. In P. Salkovskis (ed.), *Frontiers of Cognitive Therapy*. New York: Guilford Press.

Beck, A.T., Rush, A.J., Shaw, B.F. & Emery, G. (1979). *Cognitive Therapy of Depression: A Treatment Manual*. New York: Guilford Press.

Beck, A.T., Epstein, N., Brown, G. & Steer, R.A. (1988). An inventory for measuring clinical anxiety: Psychometric properties. *Journal of Consulting and Clinical Psychology*, **56**, 893–897.

Beck, A.T., Steer, R.A. & Brown, G.K. (1996). *Beck Depression Inventory-II*. San Antonio, TX: The Psychological Corporation.

Beck, A.T., Freeman, A. & Davis, D.D. (2004). *Cognitive Therapy of Personality Disorders* (2nd edn.). New York: Guilford.

Beitman, B.D. (1992). *Integration through Fundamental Similarities and Useful Differences among the Schools*. New York: Basic Books.

Bentall, R.P. (2003). *Madness Explained: Psychosis and Human Nature*. London: Allen Lane.

Berkowitz, L. (1999). Anger. In T. Dalgleish & M.J. Power (eds.), *Handbook of Cognition and Emotion*. Chichester: Wiley.

Beutler, L.E. (1991). Have all won and must all have prizes? Revisiting Luborsky et al.'s verdict. *Journal of Consulting and Clinical Psychology*, **59**, 226–232.

Blair, J., Mitchell, D. & Blair, K. (2005). *The Psychopath: Emotion and the Brain*. Oxford: Blackwell Publishing.

Bordin, E.S. (1979). The generalizability of the psychoanalytic concept of the working alliance. *Psychotherapy: Theory, Research, and Practice*, **16**, 252–260.

Borkovec, T.D. & Roehmer, L. (1995). Perceived function of worry among generalized anxiety disorder subjects: Distraction from more emotionally distressing topics? *Journal of Behavior Therapy and Experimental Psychiatry*, **26**, 25–30.

Bourdon, K.H., Boyd, J.H., Rae, D.S., Burns, B.J., Thompson, J.W. & Locke, B.Z. (1988). Gender differences in phobias: Results of the ECA community survey. *Journal of Anxiety Disorders*, **2**, 227–241.

Bower, G.H. (1981). Mood and memory. *American Psychologist*, **36**, 129–148.

Bowlby, J. (1969). *Attachment and Loss: Vol. 1, Attachment*. London: Hogarth Press.

Braam, A.W., Van Den Eeden, P., Prince, M.J., *et al.* (2001). Religion as a cross-cultural determinant of depression in elderly Europeans: Results from the EURODEP collaboration. *Psychological Medicine*, **31**, 803–814.

Breuer, J. & Freud, S. (1895/1974). Studies on hysteria. In *The Pelican Freud Library (Vol. 3)*. Harmondsworth: Penguin.

Bruner, J.S. (1983). *In Search of Mind: Essays in Autobiography*. New York: Harper Collins.

Caine, T., Wijesinghe, O. & Winter, D. (1981). *Personal Styles in Neurosis: Implications for Small Group Psychotherapy and Behaviour Therapy*. London: Routledge & Kegan Paul.

Carver, C.S. & Scheier, M.F. (1990). Origins and functions of positive and negative affect: A control process view. *Psychological Review*, **97**, 19–35.

Casement, P. (1985). *On Learning from the Patient.* London: Routledge.

Casey, R.J. (1996). *Emotional Development in Atypical Children.* Mahwah, NJ: Erlbaum.

Caspi, A., Moffitt, T.E., Newman, D.L. & Silva, P.A. (1995). Behavioural observations at age 3 years predict adult psychiatric disorders: Longitudinal evidence. *Archives of General Psychiatry*, **53**, 1033–1039.

Cavanagh, J., Schwannauer, M., Power, M.J. & Goodwin, G.M. (2009). A novel scale for measuring mixed states in bipolar disorder. *Clinical* Psychology and Psychotherapy, **16**, 497–509.

Chaiken, S. & Trope, Y. (1999) (eds.). *Dual-Process Theories in Social Psychology.* New York: Guilford Press.

Clark, D.M. (1986). A cognitive approach to panic. *Behaviour Research and Therapy*, **24**, 461–470.

Clark, D.M., Salkovskis, P.M., Hackman, A., Middleton, H., Anastasiades, P. & Gelder, M. (1994). A comparison of cognitive therapy, applied relaxation and imipramine in the treatment of panic disorder. *British Journal of Psychiatry*, **164**, 759–769.

Cooper, P.J. (1995) *Bulimia Nervosa and Binge Eating: A Guide to Recovery.* New York: New York University Press.

Dalgleish, T. & Power, M.J. (2004). Emotion specific and emotion-non-specific components of posttraumatic stress disorder (PTSD): Implications for a taxonomy of related psychopathology. *Behaviour Research and Therapy*, **42**, 1069–1088.

D'Ardenne, P. (2000). Couple and sexual problems. In L.A. Champion & M.J. Power (eds.), *Adult Psychological Problems: An Introduction.* (2nd edn.). Hove: Psychology Press.

Darwin, C. (1872/1965). *The Expression of the Emotions in Man and Animals.* Chicago: Chicago University press.

Davidson, R.J. (2000). The functional neuroanatomy of affective style. In R.D. Lane & L. Nadel (eds.), *Cognitive Neuroscience of Emotion.* New York: Oxford University Press.

Davies, M., Stankov, L. & Roberts, R.D. (1998). Emotional intelligence: In search of an elusive construct. *Journal of Personality and Social Psychology*, **75**, 989–1015.

Derakshan, N., Eysenck, M.W. & Myers, L.B. (2007). Emotional information processing in repressors: The vigilance-avoidance theory. *Cognition and Emotion*, **21**, 1585–1614.

DeRubeis, R.J., Hollon, S.D., Evans, M.D. & Bemis, K.M. (1982). Can psychotherapies for depression be discriminated? A systematic investigation of cognitive therapy and interpersonal therapy. *Journal of Consulting and Clinical Psychology*, **50**, 744–756.

Descartes, R. (1649/1989). *The Passions of the Soul.* Indianapolis, Indiana: Hackett.

DiGiuseppe, R. & Tafrate, R.C. (2007). *Understanding Anger Disorders.* Oxford: Oxford University Press.

Ekman, P. (1992). An argument for basic emotions. *Cognition and Emotion*, **6**, 169–200.

Ekman, P. (1999). Basic emotions. In T. Dalgleish & M.J. Power (eds.), *Handbook of Cognition and Emotion.* Chichester: Wiley.

Ekman, P. (2003). *Emotions Revealed: Understanding Faces and Feelings.* London: Weidenfeld and Nicolson.

Ekman, P. & Davidson, R.J. (eds.) (1994). *The Nature of Emotion: Fundamental Questions.* Oxford: Oxford University Press.

Ekman, P. Friesen, W.V. & O'Sullivan, M. (2005). Smiles when lying. In P. Ekman & E.L. Rosenberg (eds.), *What the Face Reveals* (2nd edn.). Oxford: Oxford University Press.

Ekman, P. & O'Sullivan, M. (1991). Who can catch a liar. *American Psychologist*, **46**, 913–920.

Elkin, I., Shea, M.T. & Watkins, J.T., *et al.* (1989). National Institute of Mental Health Treatment of Depression Collaborative Research program. *Archives of General Psychiatry*, **46**, 971–982.

Fairburn, C.G. (1997). Eating disorders. In D.M. Clark & C.G. Fairburn (eds.), *Science and Practice of Cognitive Behaviour Therapy.* Oxford: Oxford University Press.

Fairburn, C.G. & Beglin, S.J. (1990). The studies of the epidemiology of bulimia nervosa. *American Journal of Psychiatry*, **147**, 401–408.

Fennell, M.J.V. & Teasdale, J.D. (1987). Cognitive therapy for depression: Individual differences and the process of change. *Cognitive Therapy and Research*, **11**, 253–271.

Flavell, J.H. (1979). Metacognition and cognitive monitoring: A new area of cognitive developmental inquiry. *American Psychologist*, **34**, 906–911.

Foa, E.B. & Emmelkamp, P.M.G. (1983). *Failures in Behavior Therapy.* New York: Wiley.

Fox, J.R.E. & Harrison, A. (2008). The relation of anger to disgust: The potential role of coupled emotions within eating pathology. *Clinical Psychology and Psychotherapy*, **15**, 86–95.

Fox, J.R.E. & Power, M.J. (2009). Eating disorders and multi-level models of emotion: An integrated model. *Clinical Psychology and Psychotherapy*, **16**, 240–267.

Frank, J.D. (1982). Therapeutic components shared by all psychotherapies. In J.H. Harvey & M.M. Parks (eds.), *Psychotherapy Research and Behavior Change.* Washington, D.C.: American Psychological Association.

Freeman, C.P.L. (1998). Neurotic disorders. In E.C. Johnstone, C.P.L. Freeman & A.K. Zealley (eds.), *Companion to Psychiatric Studies* (6th edn.). Edinburgh: Churchill-Livingstone.

Freeman, C.P.L. & Power, M.J. (eds.) (2007). *Handbook of Evidence-based Psychotherapies.* Chichester: Wiley.

Freud, A. (1937). *The Ego and the Mechanisms of Defence.* London: Hogarth Press.

Freud, S. (1905). Fragment of an analysis of a case of hysteria (Dora). In *The Pelican Freud Library* (Vol. **8**). Harmondsworth: Penguin.

Freud, S. (1912). On beginning the treatment. In J. Strachey (ed.), *The Standard Edition of the Complete Psychological Works of Sigmund Freud* (Vol.**12**). London: Hogarth Press.

Freud, S. (1915/1949). The unconscious. In J. Strachey (ed. and trans.) *The Standard Edition of the Complete Psychological Works of Sigmund Freud* (Vol **14**). London: Hogarth Press.

Freud, S. (1917/1984). Mourning and melancholia. In *The Pelican Freud Library* (Vol. **11**). Harmondsworth: Penguin.

Freud, S. (1926/1979). Inhibitions, symptoms and anxiety. In *The Pelican Freud Library* (Vol. **10**). Harmondsworth: Penguin.

Frith, U. (2003). *Autism: Explaining the Enigma* (2nd edn.). Oxford: Blackwell.

Gardner, H. (1983). *Frames of Mind: The Theory of Multiple Intelligences.* New York: Basic Books.

Garfield, S.L. (1978). Research on client variables in psychotherapy. In S.L. Garfield & A.E. Bergin (eds.), *Handbook of Psychotherapy and Behavior Change: An Empirical Analysis.* (2nd edn.). New York: Wiley.

Garfield, S.L. & Bergin, A.E. (1978) (eds.). *Handbook of Psychotherapy and Behavior Change: An Empirical Analysis* (2nd edn.). New York: Wiley.

Garfield, S.L. & Bergin, A.E. (1986) (eds.). *Handbook of Psychotherapy and Behaviour Change* (3rd edn.). New York: Wiley.

Garfinkel, P.E., & Garner, D.M. (1982). *Anorexia Nervosa: A Multidimensional Perspective.* New York: Brunner Mazel.

Garfinkel, P.E., Moldofsky, H. & Garner, D.M. (1980). The heterogeneity of anorexia nervosa: Bulimia as a distinct group. *Archives of General Psychiatry*, **37**, 1036–1040.

Gaston, L., Goldfried, M.R., Greenberg, L.S., Horvath, A.O., Raue, P.J. & Watson, J. (1995). The therapeutic alliance in psychodynamic, cognitive-behavioral, and experiential therapies. *Journal of Psychotherapy Integration*, **5**, 1–26.

Goldsamt, L.A., Goldfried, M.R., Hayes, A.M. & Kerr, S. (1992). Beck, Meichenbaum, and Strupp: Comparison of three therapies on the dimension of therapist feedback. *Psychotherapy*, **29**, 167–176.

Goldstein, A.J. & Chambless, D.L. (1978). A reanalysis of agoraphobia. *Behavior Therapy*, **9**, 47–59.

Goleman, D. (1995). *Emotional Intelligence.* New York: Bantam Books.

Gray, J.A. (1982). *The Neuropsychology of Anxiety.* Oxford: Oxford University Press.

Gray, J.M., Young, A.W., Barker, W.A., Curtis, A. & Gibson, D. (1997). Impaired recognition of disgust in Huntington's disease gene carriers. *Brain*, **120**, 2029–2038.

Gross, J.J. (1998). The emerging field of emotion regulation: An integrative review. *Review of General Psychology*, **2**, 271–299.

Gross, J.J. (2007) (ed.). *Handbook of Emotion Regulation*. New York: Guilford.

Hamilton, M. (1960). A rating scale for depression. *Journal of Neurology, Neurosurgery and Psychiatry*, **25**, 56–62.

Harre, R. (1987). *The Social Construction of Emotions*. Oxford: Blackwell.

Harrington, R. (2004). Developmental perspectives on depression in young people. In M.J. Power (ed.), *Mood Disorders: A Handbook of Science and Practice*. Chichester: Wiley.

Henry, W.P., Schacht, T.E. & Strupp, H.H. (1986). Structural analysis of social behaviour: application to a study of interpersonal process in differential psychotherapeutic outcome. *Journal of Consulting and Clinical Psychology*, **54**, 27–31.

Hobson, P. (1995). *Autism and the Development of Mind*. Hove: Psychology Press.

Holmes, J. & Bateman, A. (2002). *Integration in Psychotherapy: Models and Methods*. Oxford: Oxford University Press.

Imber, S.D., Pilkonis, P.A., Sotsky, S.M., *et al.* (1990). Mode-specific effects among three treatments for depression. *Journal of Consulting and Clinical Psychology*, **58**, 352–359.

Izard, C.E. (2001). Emotional intelligence or adaptive emotions? *Emotion*, **1**, 249–257.

Izard, C.E., Libero, D.Z., Putnam, P. & Haynes, O.M. (1993). Stability of emotion experiences and their relations to traits of personality. *Journal of Personality and Social Psychology*, **64**, 847–860.

Janoff-Bulman, R. (1992). *Shattered Assumptions: Towards a New Psychology of Trauma*. New York: Free Press.

Jay, T. (2000). *Why We Curse: A Neuro-Psycho-Social Theory of Speech*. Philadelphia: John Benjamins.

Jehu, D. (1988). *Beyond Sexual Abuse: Therapy with Women Who Were Childhood Victims*. Chichester: Wiley.

Johnson-Laird, P.N. & Oatley, K. (1989). The language of emotions: An analysis of a semantic field. *Cognition and Emotion*, **3**, 81–123.

Kagan, J. (1994). *The Nature of the Child*. New York: Basic Books.

Kaplan, H.S. (1979). *Disorders of Sexual Desire*. London: Balliere Tindall.

Kaufman, G. (1989). *The Psychology of Shame: Theory and Treatment of Shame-based Syndromes*. New York: Springer.

Kendler, K.S., Maclean, C., Neale, M., *et al* (1991). The genetic epidemiology of bulimia nervosa. *American Journal of Psychiatry*, **148**, 1627–1637.

Klerman, G.L., Weissman, M.M., Rounsaville, B.J. & Chevron, E.S. (1984). *Interpersonal Psychotherapy of Depression*. New York: Basic Books.

Lam, D.H., Jones, S.H., Hayward, P. & Bright, J.A. (1999). *Cognitive Therapy for Bipolar Disorder*. Chichester: Wiley.

Lambert, M.J. (2004) (ed.). *Bergin and Garfield's Handbook of Psychotherapy and Behavior Change*. New York: Wiley.

Larsen, R.J. (2000). Toward a science of mood regulation. *Psychological Inquiry*, **11**, 129–141.

LeDoux, J.E. (1996). *The Emotional Brain: The Mysterious Underpinnings of Emotional Life.* New York: Simon & Schuster.

Leventhal, H. & Scherer, K. (1987). The relationship of emotion to cognition: A functional approach to a semantic controversy. *Cognition and Emotion*, **1**, 3–28.

Lewis, M. (2000). The emergence of human emotions. In M. Lewis & J.M. Haviland-Jones (eds.), *Handbook of Emotions.* (2nd edn.). New York: Guilford.

Linehan, M.M. (1993). *Cognitive-Behavioral Treatment of Borderline Personality Disorder.* New York: Guilford.

Livesley, W.J. (2001). *Handbook of Personality Disorders: Theory, Research, and Treatment.* New York: Guilford.

Luborsky, L., Woody, G.E., Mclellan, A.T., O'Brien, C.P. & Rosenweig, J. (1982). Can independent judges recognise different psychotherapies? An experience with manual-guided therapies. *Journal of Consulting and Clinical Psychology*, **50**, 49–62.

Luborsky, L., Mclellan, A.T., Woody, G.E., O'Brien, C.P. & Auerbach, A. (1985). Therapist success and its determinants. *Archives of General Psychiatry*, **42**, 602–611.

Lutz, C.A. (1988). *Unnatural Emotions: Everyday Sentiments on a Micronesian Atoll and Their Challenge to Western Theory.* Chicago: University of Chicago Press.

Marks, I.M. (1969). *Fears and Phobias.* New York: Academic Press.

Miller, W.R., Westerberg, V.S., Harris, R.J. & Tonigan, J.S. (1996). What predicts relapse? Prospective testing of antecedent models. *Addiction*, **91** (Suppl), 155–172.

Mitchell, J. & McCarthy, H. (2000). Eating disorders. In L.A. Champion & M.J. Power (eds.), *Adult Psychological Problems: An Introduction.* (2nd edn.). Hove: Psychology Press.

Myers, J.K., Weissman, M.M., Tischler, G.L., *et al.* (1984). Six-month prevalence of psychiatric disorders in three communities. *Archives of General Psychiatry*, **41**, 959–967.

Nisbett, R.E. & Wilson, T.D. (1977). Telling more than we can know: Verbal reports on mental processes. *Psychological Review*, **84**, 231–259.

Norcross, J.C. & Goldfried, M.R. (1992). *Handbook of Psychotherapy Integration.* New York: Basic Books.

Oatley, K. (2004). *Emotions: A Brief History.* Oxford: Blackwell.

Oatley, K. & Duncan, E. (1992). Incidents of emotion in daily life. In K.T. Strongman (ed.), *International Review of Studies on Emotion* (Vol. **2**). Chichester: Wiley.

Oatley, K. & Johnson-Laird, P.N. (1987). Towards a cognitive theory of emotions. *Cognition and Emotion*, **1**, 29–50.

O'Brien, C.P., Ehrman, R.E. & Ternes, J.W. (1986). Classical conditioning in human opioid dependence. In S.R. Goldberg & I.P. Stolerman (eds.), *Behavioural Analysis of Drug Dependence*. San Diego, CA: Academic Press.

Osgood, C.E., Suci, G.J. & Tannenbaum, P.H. (1957). *The Measurement of Meaning*. Urbana, IL: University of Illinois.

Pennebaker, J.W. (1982). *The Psychology of Physical Symptoms*. New York: Springer-Verlag.

Philippot, P. (2007). *Emotion et Psychotherapie*. Wavre: Mardaga.

Philippot, P. & Feldman, R.S. (2004) (eds.). *The Regulation of Emotion*. Mahwah, NJ: Erlbaum.

Phillips, K.F.V. & Power, M.J. (2007). A new self-report measure of emotion regulation in adolescents: The Regulation of Emotions Questionnaire. *Clinical Psychology and Psychotherapy*, **14**, 145–156.

Plato (1953). *The Timaeus* [B. Jowett trans.]. Oxford: Oxford University Press.

Powell, J. (1995). Classical responses to drug-related stimuli: Is context crucial? *Addiction*, **90**, 1089–1095.

Powell, J. (2000). Drug and alcohol dependence. In L.A. Champion & M.J. Power (eds.), *Adult Psychological Problems: An Introduction*. (2nd edn.). Hove: Psychology Press.

Power, M.J. (1991). Cognitive science and behavioural psychotherapy: Where behaviour was, there shall cognition be? *Behavioural Psychotherapy*, **19**, 20–41.

Power, M.J. (1997). Conscious and unconscious representations of meaning. In M.J. Power & C.R. Brewin (eds.), *The Transformation of Meaning in Psychological Therapies*. Chichester: Wiley.

Power, M.J. (1999). Sadness and its disorders. In T. Dalgleish & M.J. Power (eds.), *Handbook of Cognition and Emotion*. Chichester: Wiley.

Power, M.J. (2001). Memories of abuse and alien abduction: Close encounters of the therapeutic kind. In Davies, G.M. and Dalgleish, T. (eds.), *Recovered Memories: Seeking the Middle Ground*. Chichester: Wiley.

Power, M.J. (2002). Integrative therapy from a cognitive-behavioural perspective. In J. Holmes & A. Bateman (2002), *Integration in Psychotherapy: Models and Methods*. Oxford: Oxford University Press.

Power, M.J. (2003). Quality of life. In S. Snyder & S. Lopez (eds.), *Handbook of Positive Psychological Assessment*. Washington. D.C.: American Psychological Association.

Power, M.J. (2005). Psychological approaches to bipolar disorders: A theoretical critique. *Clinical Psychology Review*, **25**, 1101–1122.

Power, M.J. (2006). The structure of emotion: An empirical comparison of six models. *Cognition and Emotion*, **20**, 694–713.

Power, M.J. (2007). The multistory self: Why the self is more than the sum of its autoparts. *Journal of Clinical Psychology*, **63**, 187–198.

Power, M.J., Champion, L.A. & Aris, S.J. (1988). The development of a measure of social support: The Significant Others (SOS) Scale. *British Journal of Clinical Psychology*, **27**, 349–358.

Power, M.J. & Cheung, H.N.. The measure of depression, (in prep).

Power, M.J. & Dalgleish, T. (1997). *Cognition and Emotion: From Order to Disorder*. Hove: Erlbaum.

Power, M.J. & Dalgleish, T. (1999). Two routes to emotion: Some implications of multi-level theories of emotion for therapeutic practice. *Behavioural and Cognitive Psychotherapy*, **27**, 129–141.

Power, M.J. & Dalgleish, T. (2008). *Cognition and Emotion: From Order to Disorder* (2nd edn.). Hove: Erlbaum.

Power, M.J., Katz, R., McGuffin, P., Duggan, C.F., Lam, D. & Beck, A.T. (1994). The Dysfunctional Attitude Scale (DAS): A comparison of forms A and B and proposals for a new subscaled version. *Journal of Research in Personality*, **28**, 263–276.

Power M.J. & Freeman, C.P.L. (2007). Introduction. In C.P.L. Freeman & M.J. Power (eds.), *Handbook of Evidence-based Psychotherapies*. Chichester: Wiley.

Power, M.J. & Tarsia, M. (2007). Basic and complex emotions in depression and anxiety. *Clinical Psychology and Psychotherapy*, **14**, 19–31.

Prochaska, J.O. & Diclemente, C.C. (1992). The transtheoretical approach. In J.C. Norcross & M.G. Goldfried (eds.), *Handbook of Psychotherapy Integration*. New York: Basic Books.

Rachman, S.J. (1990). *Fear and Courage* (2nd edn.). New York: W.H. Freeman.

Rachman, S.J. (2003). *The Treatment of Obsessions*. Oxford: Oxford University Press.

Rachman, S.J. (2004). *Anxiety*. (2nd edn.). Hove: Psychology Press.

Rachman, S.J. & De Silva, P. (1996). *Panic Disorder: The Facts*. Oxford: Oxford University Press.

Richards, D.A., Lovell, K. & Marks, I.M. (1994). Post-traumatic stress disorder: Evaluation of a behavioral treatment program. *Journal of Traumatic Stress*, **7**, 669–680.

Roberts, R.D., Zeidner, M. & Matthews, G. (2001). Does emotional intelligence meet traditional standards for intelligence? Some new data and conclusions. *Emotion*, **1**, 196–231.

Robinson, L.A., Berman, J.S. & Neimeyer, R.A. (1990). Psychotherapy for the treatment of depression: A comprehensive review of controlled outcome research. *Psychological Bulletin*, **108**, 30–49.

Robson, P. (1989). Development of a new self-report questionnaire to measure self-esteem. *Psychological Medicine*, **19**, 513–518.

Rogers, C.R. (1957). The necessary and sufficient conditions of therapeutic personality change. *Journal of Consulting Psychology*, **21**, 95–103.

Rolls, E.T. (1999). *The Brain and Emotion*. Oxford: Oxford University Press.

Rozin, P. & Fallon, A.E. (1987). A perspective on disgust. *Psychological Review*, **94**, 23–41.

Rozin, P., Haidt, J. & McCauley, C.R. (1999). Disgust: The body and soul emotion. In T. Dalgleish & M.J. Power (eds.), *Handbook of Cognition and Emotion*. Chichester: Wiley.

Russell, G.F.M. (1970). Anorexia nervosa: Its identity as an illness and its treatment. In J.H. Price (ed.), *Modern Trends in Psychological Medicine* (Vol. **2**). London: Butterworths.

Russell, G.F.M. (1979). Bulimia nervosa: An ominous variant of anorexia nervosa. *Psychological Medicine*, **9**, 429–448.

Russell, J. (1994). Is there universal recognition of emotion from facial expression? A review of the cross-cultural studies. *Psychological Bulletin*, **115**, 102–141.

Russell, J.A. & Carroll, J.M. (1999). On the bipolarity of positive and negative affect. *Psychological Bulletin*, **125**, 3–30.

Rutter, M. (1994). Beyond longitudinal data: Causes, consequences, changes and continuity. *Journal of Consulting and Clinical Psychology*, **62**, 928–940.

Safran, J.D. & Segal, Z.V. (1990). *Interpersonal Process in Cognitive Therapy*. New York: Basic Books.

Salkovskis, P.M. (1985). Obsessional-compulsive problems: A cognitive-behavioural analysis. *Behaviour Research and Therapy*, **23**, 571–583.

Salovey, P. & Mayer, J.D. (1990). Emotional intelligence. *Imagination, Cognition, and Personality*, **9**, 185–211.

Scherer, K.R., Schorr, A. & Johnstone, T. (2001) (eds.). *Appraisal Processes in Emotion: Theory, Methods, Research*. Oxford: Oxford University Press.

Schwannauer, M. & Power, M.J.. Psychotherapy for bipolar disorder, in preparation.

Segal, Z.V., Williams, J.M.G. & Teasdale, J.D. (2001). *Mindfulness-based Cognitive Therapy for Depression: A New Approach to Preventing Relapse*. New York: Guilford.

Shapiro, D.A., Firth-Cozens, J. & Stiles, W.B. (1989). The question of therapists' differential effectiveness: A Sheffield Psychotherapy Project addendum. *British Journal of Psychiatry*, **154**, 383–385.

Shaw, B.F. & Wilson-Smith, D. (1988). Training therapists in cognitive-behaviour therapy. In C. Perris, I.M. Blackburn & H. Perris (eds.), *Cognitive Psychotherapy: Theory and Practice*. Berlin: Springer-Verlag.

Sloane, R.B., Staples, F.R., Cristol, A.H., Yorkston, N.J. & Whipple, K. (1975). *Psychotherapy Versus Behaviour Therapy*. Cambridge, MA: Harvard University Press.

Spielberger, C.D. (1983). *Manual for the State-Trait Anxiety Inventory (Form Y)*. Palo Alto, CA: Consulting Psychologists Press.

Stieper, D.R. & Wiener, D.N. (1959). The problem of interminability in outpatient psychotherapy. *Journal of Consulting Psychology*, **23**, 237–242.

Stiles, W.B., Shapiro, D.A. & Elliott, R. (1986). Are all psychotherapies equivalent? *American Psychologist*, **41**, 165–180.

Stiles, W.B., Elliott, R., Llewelyn, S.P., *et al.* (1990). Assimilation of problematic experiences by clients in psychotherapy. *Psychotherapy*, **27**, 411–420.

Stroebe, M.S., Hansson, R.O., Stroebe, W. & Schut, H. (2001) (eds.). *Handbook of Bereavement Research*. Washington, D.C.: American Psychological Association.

Stuart, S. & Robertson, M. (2003). *Interpersonal Psychotherapy: A Clinician's Guide*. London: Hodder Arnold.

Talwar, V., Gordon, H.M. & Lee, K. (2007). Lying in the elementary school years: Verbal deception and its relation to second-order belief understanding. *Developmental Psychology*, **43**, 804–810.

Tangney, J.P. (1999). The self-conscious emotions: Shame, guilt, embarrassment and pride. In T. Dalgleish & M.J. Power (eds.), *Handbook of Cognition and Emotion*. Chichester: Wiley.

Taylor, G.J. (2001). Low emotional intelligence and mental health. In J. Ciarrochi, J.P. Forgas & J.D. Mayer (eds.), *Emotional Intelligence in Everyday Life: A Scientific Inquiry*. Philadelphia: Psychology Press.

Taylor, G.J., Bagby, R.M. & Parker, J.D.A. (1997). *Disorders of Affect Regulation: Alexithymia in Medical and Psychiatric Illness*. Cambridge: Cambridge University Press.

Teasdale, J.D. (1983). Negative thinking in depression: Cause, effect, or reciprocal relationship? *Advances in Behaviour Research and Therapy*, **5**, 3–25.

Teasdale, J.D. (1999). Multi-level theories of cognition-emotion relations. In T. Dalgleish & M.J. Power (eds.), *Handbook of Cognition and Emotion*. Chichester: Wiley.

Teasdale, J. & Barnard, P. (1993). *Affect, Cognition and Change*. Hove: Erlbaum.

Truax, C.B. & Carkhuff, R.R. (1967). *Toward Effective Counselling and Psychotherapy: Training and Practice*. Chicago: Aldine.

Vaillant, G.E. (1990). Repression in college men followed for half a century. In J.L. Singer (ed.), *Repression and Dissociation*. Chicago: University of Chicago Press.

Vaillant, G.E. (2002). *Ageing Well*. Oxford: Blackwell Publishing.

Waller, G. (1992). Sexual abuse and the severity of bulimic symptoms. *British Journal of Psychiatry*, **161**, 90–93.

Watson, D. & Clark, L.A. (1992). Affects separable and inseparable: On the hierarchical arrangement of the negative affects. *Journal of Personality and Social Psychology*, **62**, 489–505.

Watson, D., Clark, L.A. & Tellegen, A. (1988). Development and validation of brief measures of positive and negative affect: The PANAS scales. *Journal of Personality and Social Psychology*, **54**, 1063–1070.

Wegner, D.M. (1994). Ironic processes of mental control. *Psychological Review*, **101**, 34–52.

Weinberger, D.A., Schwartz, G.E. & Davidson. R.J. (1979). Low-anxious, high anxious and repressive coping styles: Psychometric patterns and behavioural responses to stress. *Journal of Abnormal Psychology*, **88**, 369–380.

Weissman, M.M., Markowitz, J.C. & Klerman, G.L. (2000). *Comprehensive Guide to Interpersonal Psychotherapy*. New York: Basic Books.

Wittenbrink, B. & Schwarz, N. (2007). *Implicit Measures of Attitudes: Procedures and Controversies*. New York: Guilford.

Wolfe, B.E. & Goldfried, M.R. (1988). Research on psychotherapy integration: Recommendations and conclusions from an NIMH workshop. *Journal of Consulting and Clinical Psychology*, **56**, 448–451.

Wolpe, J. (1958). *Psychotherapy by Reciprocal Inhibition*. Stanford, CA: Stanford University Press.

World Health Organisation (1979). *Schizophrenia: An International Follow-up Study*. New York: Wiley.

Young, J.E. (1999). *Cognitive Therapy for Personality Disorders: A Schema-focused Approach* (Rev. edn.). Sarasota, FL: Professional Resources Press.

Zigmond, A.S. & Snaith, R.P. (1983). The Hospital Anxiety and Depression Scale. *Acta Psychiatrica Scandinavica*, **67**, 361–370.

Zimbardo, P. (2007). *The Lucifer Effect: How Good People Turn Evil*. London: Rider.

Author Index

Subject Index